KU-216-722

Reality
beyond
Reason

The story of TELit

Barry Sprott

THEMATIC EVANGELISTIC LITERATURE

Barry Sprott, founder and General Manager of TELit has served for a number of years as an Elder in Charlotte Baptist Chapel, Edinburgh. Following a career in social work, Barry established the ministry of TELit in 1990. Through its range of full colour thematic evangelistic folders the aim has been to communicate faithfully the essential elements of the gospel in a contemporary style and format, thus demonstrating the relevance of the message for today. Since its formation around 15,000,000 outreach folders have been circulated worldwide.

I do hope you'll enjoy this book in which I've done my best to ensure accuracy and sensitivity. However, if as a result of reading it you're left feeling disappointed, offended or upset in any other way, please accept my sincere apologies. After all, I claim to be no more than just an ordinary, everyday sinner saved by grace.

Barry Sprott

Please note that throughout this book the representation of TELit folder front covers is not to scale.

Typesetting and page assembly by Lorraine Agnew
Cover Design by Ken Macindoe

Reprinted by permission. 'The Sacred Romance' (p 107) Brent Curtis and John Eldredge,1997 Thomas Nelson Inc. Nashville, Tennessee. All rights reserved. 'Keep up the good work' (p 172) is courtesy of Dennis J De Hann, Our Daily Bread, copyright ©1991 by RBC Ministries, Grand Rapids, Michigan, USA.

All Scripture quotations, in this publication are from the HOLY BIBLE, NEW INTERNATIONAL VERSION (r) NIV (r) Copyright (c) 1973, 1978, 1984 by Biblica, Inc.(tm). All rights reserved worldwide.

Copyright ©TELit 2010
ISBN 978-0-9566448-0-0

Published in 2010 by The Thematic Evangelistic Literature Co Ltd
144a Ferry Road, EDINBURGH EH6 4NX, Scotland
Tel: 0131 554 0339   Fax: 0131 554 2330
E-mail: info@telitquick.org   Website: www.telitquick.org

All rights reserved. No part of this publication may be reproduced, stored in a retrieval system, or transmitted in any form, by any means, electronic, mechanical, photocopying, recording or otherwise without the prior permission of the publisher or a licence permitting restricted copying. In the U.K. such licences are issued by the Copyright Licensing Agency, Saffron House, 6-10 Kirby Street, London, EC1 8TS   www.cla.co.uk

INTRODUCTION

I've often been asked to give some explanation as to how and why TELit came into being. So, I've put together this brief history of its origins and development before Olde Father Tyme has thoroughly ravaged my recollections.

But if this were to form merely a factual record, interesting though it might be to some, I would rather have spent my time and energy writing more evangelistic literature, listening to love songs from the 60's and watching old episodes of 'Hill Street Blues'!

Instead of simply charting the many highs and lows since the establishment of the work in 1990, I do hope that this publication will pay tribute to the incredible grace of our Lord and Saviour, Jesus Christ. He is the founder of the work and I trust also, the true author of every TELit publication. The message is His, and if lives have been changed and destinies secured through the printed page, then it is because He has chosen to work in this way.

Although I have been the central figure in its origins and development, TELit is by no means a 'one man show'. From the very beginning it's been a real team effort. Many people have contributed significantly to the success of the work, and it would be impossible not to make reference to some in this book. Yet many more get no mention whatsoever, though I suspect that most, if not all, are happy for this to be the case. I have the feeling however that those who have played their part in a quiet, unassuming way, though anonymous to you, are well known to heaven.

So come, let me take you on a rather unusual journey. One full of twists and turns, ups and downs, but which has, in the providence of God, proved a 'Reality beyond Reason'.

Barry Sprott, Autumn 2010

Living in the Seafield area of Kirkcaldy, I and my friends spent many happy hours riding our bikes, beachcombing along the shore and building ganghuts on some of the derelict land nearby.

And now, more than 50 years on, it's wonderful to hear from Myra Thomson (now Wishart) and Linda Williamson (now Gorham) - courtesy of social networking sites - and I treasure the fun we have reliving precious memories from past times.

As a family I suppose we would have been considered very ordinary by worldly standards. Each of us went through periods of poor health; money was always very tight, and family tensions would rear their ugly heads from time to time. And yet my sister and I have always been very grateful for the love and care that formed a solid foundation for all that was to lie ahead in later life.

My dad

SCHOOL DAYS

School began for me at the age of five but within a few years Abbotshall Primary closed down. This meant adjustment to a new situation altogether at Kirkcaldy West... and a much longer walk for little legs!

I scraped through the Eleven Plus exam and found myself at Kirkcaldy High School, in the same year as Prime Minister-to-be Gordon Brown. This school had a glowing reputation for outstanding academic achievement. And therefore, had the educational powers that be ever noticed me, which they never did, I would have proved a great disappointment to them. In fact I struggled my way through the first couple of years until 1963 when my family had to move through to the west of Scotland because of my father's work.

My first day at Dumbarton Academy happened to be my 14th birthday, and from that point on, school became a much less miserable experience. Not only did I begin to find the work more

9

manageable, but I enjoyed playing football for the school, as well as the thrill of forming romantic attachments!

That's me, 2nd from the left in the back row, playing for Dumbarton Academy

However, less than two years on, we had to move back to Kirkcaldy, as a result of changing family circumstances. This meant a return to the dreaded Kirkcaldy High. In those days there wasn't much by way of 'pastoral' concern within the Secondary Education system, and with no national curriculum, I found the differences between the schools just too much to handle. I lost heart academically, had disastrous results in my 'O' grade prelims, and sorely missed the lovely girl I'd left behind in Dumbarton. It actually felt something of a relief when I was summoned to the Headmaster's office and told to leave. It was a 'survival of the fittest' regime and I had failed miserably.

I left school with no academic qualifications whatsoever and can honestly say that, in contrast to Gordon Brown, I hated every day at Kirkcaldy High. In fact, my happiest school day was undoubtedly my last one!

EARLY CHRISTIAN INFLUENCE

My parents were members of the Church of Scotland and, as was normal in the '50's, we attended pretty regularly. My sister and I went to Sunday School and Bible Class, but on moving to Dumbarton in '63 we failed to make any meaningful connections

10

with a local church. All too readily I welcomed the opportunity to spend Sundays playing football down at Dumbarton Castle or

with school friends in the Cafe Continental on the Glasgow Road.

Returning to Kirkcaldy we picked up the threads of involvement in our previous church, Bethelfield, especially as many of the congregation were long-standing family friends. By this time however I was struggling to see how Christianity - which seemed to me to amount to little more

Lang Toun Lass Anne Renton (now Easson) and me

than a plea to follow a set of moral principles - would answer a growing sense of emptiness at the heart of my life.

Yet my teenage years were far from dull. I became involved for a while with another Church of Scotland in the town, St Brycedale's. This was where Gordon Brown's father was the Minister, and his older brother, John, the inspirational leader of the young people. Through this I was introduced to 'Operation Friendship', an international youth exchange. I became a member of the Junior Chamber of Commerce; spent a brief

Appearing in 'The Gypsy Baron' with Markinch Amateur Operatic Society

time with Raith Rovers youth team; had great fun taking part in 8 local amateur operatic shows, and was even elected Kirkcaldy's 'Lang Toun Lad' in 1969! And yet still there seemed to be something missing - a deep yearning for something.

Although immediate and extended family members were not of an evangelical persuasion, they did firmly believe in the importance of basic Christian principles. And this is something

11

for which I've always been very grateful.

I was to realise in days to come that they were immersed, as had been their parents before them, in a church scene very different from the one I was to discover in 1974. Through my own Church of Scotland involvement in Fife I got to know many warm, caring, sincere people, who were living honest and decent lives. Yet I wonder if there had been others like me, hungering for a deeper, and more meaningful spiritual reality. When reflecting upon this possibility, the well-known line from Milton's 'Lycidas' comes to mind, *'The hungry sheep look up, and are not fed.'*

In those days however spiritual matters seemed to be considered a largely personal and private concern. They were rarely a topic of everyday conversation, especially amongst older people.

Even at school, where in the early 60's Scotland was at least a nominally Christian country, political correctness was still to be invented and there was yet to be a legal requirement to teach comparative religions, surely we could have been given the basic doctrines of mainstream Christianity. But no, just dry moral philosophising as far as I can remember.

Kirkcaldy High School

Even if my RE teachers could have professed little personal faith, at least we could have been given a handout detailing the essential elements of the gospel...

12

I didn't realise it at the time of course, but in years to come I was to see the Lord's hand in this key milestone in my life. This lucky break, as I was considering it, was really the Lord manoeuvring me into a line of work which would form something of a foundation for much more than I could ever imagine.

THE WORLD OF WORK

As I entered the world of work I was suddenly faced with a very steep learning curve. My job involved setting out the details and technical specification of each order and overseeing their safe passage through the various stages of production. Much of my working day was also spent in telephone communication with customers, for many of whom I was the main point of contact with the Company.

So it was really from 1966 that I began to gain an appreciation of just how noble is the printing industry, epitomised by the following plaque which was displayed on the wall of our office...

> # THIS
> ## IS A PRINTING OFFICE.
>
> Crossroads of civilization. Refuge of all the arts against the ravages of time. Armory of fearless truth against whispering rumor. Incessant trumpet of trade. From this place words may fly abroad, not to perish on waves of sound, not to vary with the writer's hand but fixed in time, having been verified in proof. *Friend you stand on sacred ground,*
>
> This is a Printing Office.

Not only did I have to undergo a crash course in the realm of technical knowledge, I even needed to learn how to use the telephone, never having had one in my home up until this point. Another tough test for me was learning to cultivate the art of diplomacy, which was to be required in great measure, as I found myself having to appease impatient customers who had unrealistic expectations of the production process. I also had to 'negotiate' with hard-bitten foremen, a number of whom were prone to becoming particularly aggressive when under pressure!

I found all this immensely challenging. But once again I was to look back in years to come and acknowledge how the Lord was orchestrating my circumstances for purposes which were to lie well ahead in the future.

The Allen Lithographic Co. Ltd. in Kirkcaldy, shown from the rear

For example, I was fascinated to see how the girls in our Dispatch Department could count printed items by hand as quickly as they did. And simply as a bit of fun, I got them to teach me their technique. For the following 24 years I did nothing with this new found skill... until TELit came along and then it proved absolutely essential!

After 4 years as the Company's order and progress clerk I was ready for a change. So it was to my sheer delight that I was offered the opportunity to become one of the firm's sales reps in 1970. And being given a company car at the age of 20, which I could also use in my own time, opened up a whole new world of possibility to me! Needless to say I grasped this opportunity with both hands, though much of what I got up to over the next few years is now best forgotten as it was far from honouring to the Lord.

16

And so here I encountered what was for me a totally new phenomenon. I had never even heard of such a thing before and yet suddenly I was in the midst of one! There must have been close on 100 participants of all ages, offering audible, spontaneous but orderly prayers. Had I stumbled across some weird cult of fanatics?

If this was authentic, mainstream Christianity it was most certainly of a variety I had never seen before. Up until this point my perception of 'Church' was that of an institution which was just so 'last century' and had drifted to the very margins of contemporary society. To my mind, it was a relic from bygone days that was rapidly outliving its usefulness and where those who struggled to cope with life sought a crutch. It was where elderly people prepared for their 'finals' and Ministers were glorified community workers. And while in days gone by churches converted sinners, now sinners were converting churches.

This new church experience took me well and truly out of my comfort zone. Yet many aspects of it made a favourable impression upon me. And perhaps most unexpected of all, though it challenged my firmly held stereotypes, I felt strangely drawn to the people and what they appeared to stand for.

ON REFLECTION

As I look back upon this particular week in my life, I'm so glad that Maureen didn't compromise her Christian convictions. If so, things could well have worked out quite differently. I'm not suggesting of course that the Lord's overall plan for me may have been thwarted, but as I hardly appeared the 'religious type' it took a fair amount of courage on Maureen's part to take me to a prayer meeting, thus leaving me in no doubt as to her beliefs. This proved to be my most unlikely first date ever! But then, which one of us knows how the Lord is working in someone else's heart and what might make a significant spiritual impact upon their lives. Each of us is made by Him, for a relationship with Him, and at this stage in my life only He knew how close I was to the decisive tipping point.

Chapter 4

Unconditional Surrender

'If anyone is in Christ, he is a new creation; the old has gone, the new has come!'

2 Corinthians 5:17

I found this whole new church scene somewhat unsettling to say the least. But I was struck by the obvious sincerity of these people and especially their concern for the spiritual well-being of others. Although I was sufficiently intrigued to go back for more throughout the week, I felt very strongly to have been on the outside of something, looking in. During this time Maureen and her friends answered all my many questions honestly and sincerely, whilst at the same time not putting any pressure upon me whatsoever.

It was becoming clear to me that for the folks at Charlotte Chapel, the Lord had first place in their lives. So it came as no real surprise when, on the Thursday evening of that week, Maureen told me, in the nicest possible way, she reckoned that as things stood, there was really no future for our relationship. I was beginning to realise this myself and knew in my heart of hearts that unless one of us changed then what she said was perfectly correct. And yet I saw so much that I admired in Maureen that I didn't want her to be the one to change.

CONSIDERING THE COST

The next day my mind was in turmoil. Throughout the week I'd felt as though I was being faced with having to make a decision, and now things were coming to a head. Yet one thing was quite clear to me, this decision was between me and God, and would have profound implications. Whether or not Maureen was to figure in my future was somehow of secondary importance. (For once I was about to exercise genuine integrity with regard to a young lady.)

GRATITUDE - If I was to be facing a terminal illness and one day discovered some way by which I could be completely cured, wouldn't I want to share this 'good news' with others facing the same predicament? Discovering the way of salvation is surely all the more important as the life we live in this world is but a drop in a bucket when compared to Eternity!

LOVE - Life is all about relationships. And if as professing Christians we're facing up to the challenge of loving our neighbour as ourselves, we can't ignore the importance of sharing the gospel with them. I really believe that the essence of true love is seeking the best for the other person. And if so, surely the very best we can do for someone else is to help see them come to saving faith in the Lord Jesus Christ, through our words as well as our unspoken witness.

COMPULSION - The Apostle Paul refers to having been 'compelled by the Spirit', and I have to say that I too share the same sense of spiritual pressure. But this is not the result of guilt, duty, or the hope of gaining some form of altruistic 'Brownie points' ...perish the very thought! I felt, and continue to feel, the fire of passion that people might receive the wonderful truth of the gospel, while there's still time.

Of course, not all Christians have the gift of evangelism, but we are all called to be witnesses. Facing up to this realisation I began recognising opportunities, mainly at work. I found that colleagues were often much more open to discuss such things than I had previously imagined.

In fact, during my time with the RSSPCC and later in the Social Work Department, I had many conversations of a spiritual nature over lunch, during coffee breaks, or whilst driving with a colleague. I was in the habit of asking the Lord every morning for an opportunity to say something of spiritual value that day. Time and time again this prayer was answered in the affirmative, though I would usually respond to colleagues' questions with a fair bit of trepidation.

Chapter 6

Life at the Sharp End

'I can do everything through him who gives me strength.'

Philippians 4:13

On 26th April 1974 I had asked Christ Jesus into my life by His Spirit to become my personal Lord and Saviour. As a result I was now like a shop bearing the sign, 'Under New Management'.

I went on to discover that in the Bible we're told that God has a life-plan for each of us and therefore it seemed very important for me to be clear as to whether or not I was in the right employment. Following a period of training I had been appointed the Inspector for Pilton, Granton and Leith, an area with a population of around 50,000! I had some serious misgivings as to my suitability for work with the RSSPCC, but though I committed this matter to Him in prayer no specific sign appeared to direct me elsewhere. In view of this I got my head down and with His help set out to be the best I could be in the investigation of alleged incidents of non-accidental injury and neglect.

Maureen had begun her two year professional qualification in Social Work at Robert Gordon's College in Aberdeen and during her time away from Edinburgh I thought I should try to get some academic qualifications as well. So I enrolled at Boroughmuir Commercial Institute (night school) where, as a rather mature student of 25, I managed to get 'O' grade English and Arithmetic, with Higher English at Telford College the following year.

WORKING FOR THE RSSPCC

I found my work as a RSSPCC Inspector extremely difficult and often quite harrowing. In those days West Pilton was considered amongst the most deprived and crime-ridden housing estates in Western Europe. And as I was never a popular visitor for those upon whom I had to call, I'm sure it was only by the Lord's grace that I managed to survive such visits physically unscathed! During my time with the RSSPCC I was the only Inspector within the Edinburgh office not to have been physically assaulted. Yet each day brought potential hazards of one sort or another. On one occasion a young mother aimed a kiss at me and it was only through the speed of my body swerve and degree of her inebriation that she missed!

Back in the mid 70's drug addiction wasn't nearly as prevalent as it is today. It was the widespread abuse of alcohol which lay behind so much of the violence, family upheaval and misery that I encountered every day. And of course it's the children who are usually the real losers in such situations. At this critical stage in their development they crave love and security, warmth, fun and understanding. Yet the adults in their household, who for them are giants controlling every aspect of their lives, are all too often inconsistent, unpredictable and at one another's throats - sometimes literally.

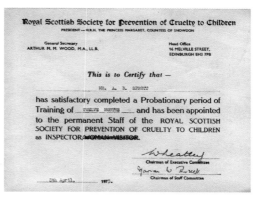

RSSPCC Certificate of Appointment

As a young unmarried man with no children of my own, I was also an easy target for a fair bit of aggression, from mothers in particular. And of course to find a RSSPCC Inspector standing on the doorstep was a most alarming experience - once it was realised who I was. When introducing myself as from the RSSPCC I had to expect some confusion and was often ready with the words, *'No, it's no the dug, it's the bairns!'* My lack of child-rearing experience in particular would often put me on the back foot. However, I would resort to reminding the mother in question that I'd been a child myself. And I knew I would certainly not like to have been left in the same nappy all day or had my hand burnt with a cigarette!

MARRIAGE AND A NEW JOB

In September 1976, with Maureen having completed her training and our romance having survived the enforced separation, we were delighted to become Mr and Mrs. She had been seconded on to her course by the Social Work Department and consequently returned to work in the Craigmillar area. I continued with 'the Cruelty' (slang name for the RSSPCC) and completed over 100 investigations into allegations of child abuse. Then, out of the blue, a timely opportunity arose for me to transfer to the Social Work Department. This move seemed a natural progression as it promised to give me a wider theoretical perspective on the personal social services. Although I had no formal social work training, I was taken on in view of the experience I had gained with the RSSPCC. In fact, over those two years or so, I had been involved in more child protection work than anyone else in the Pilton social work team I was set to join.

Two years on and I was also seconded by the Department to undergo professional training. I was accepted by Queen Margaret College in Edinburgh on the basis of my practical experience and night school qualifications. Little did I know that 30 years into the future, my youngest daughter Rebekah would study Event Management with the same

QUEEN MARGARET COLLEGE
EDINBURGH

DIPLOMA IN SOCIAL WORK

This is to certify that

BARRY SPROTT

completed a two year full-time course at the College and was awarded this Diploma which is recognised by the Central Council for Education and Training in Social Work

Chairman David J. Mauri
Principal Claudine L. Megson   Date 9 October 1979

Social Work Qualification

institution, now elevated to University status.

Although I was hardly a high flyer I managed to negotiate the course with no re-sits. This was despite an exhilarating year as leader of the Christian Union and becoming something of an expert on the table football machine in the Student Union.

Following qualification in 1979 I worked for the Department in a variety of settings for a further 15 years. In addition to spells in the Musselburgh and Oxgangs area offices, I enjoyed having special responsibility for services to adolescents in the West Division comprising Gorgie/Dalry, Muirhouse and Wester Hailes. My final post with Lothian Regional Council was that of Resource Team Manager, overseeing substitute family care (mainly fostering and adoption) in the North East quarter of the City, better known as Leith.

During these years I was also given the opportunity to do several time-limited jobs at Departmental Headquarters. One involved being appointed a locum for the Information, Education and Publicity Officer during the incumbent's year of absence. This meant that instead of writing reports for the courts or Children's Hearing System, I was now faced with, amongst many other things, having to produce press releases and take responsibility for compiling and designing the Department's many and varied publications. Thankfully the team I managed was full of ability and I learned a lot from

Social Work Department Publicity and Education Officer

them. This work was something of a new venture for me but looking back I can see that it formed part of the preparation the Lord was giving me for future work. And the fact that I had been head-hunted for the post was perhaps not without significance.

Nevertheless, I do often wonder why the Lord had me work in the social services for what were probably the best years of my life. I say this because I consider the work of the gospel through TELit to be by far the most important work I've ever done, given the profundity of its eternal significance. Maybe it was to ensure that Maureen and I would have a bit of a pension into, God willing, our old age. But perhaps, more seriously, it was to leave me in no doubt whatsoever, as to the nature of the human condition, as well as the limitations of man-made solutions. But please don't get me wrong, I have no doubts as to the true value of social work. The social services form a daily lifeline for so many. Yet, the countless success stories up and down the country don't sell newspapers! Sadly it's the occasions on which things go wrong that hit the headlines and the poor social worker is much maligned once again. Though none of us would want to excuse sloppy professional practice, until we've been *on the inside* in such circumstances, it's all too easy to criticise and condemn prematurely.

Throughout my years in the social services, I've seen enough misery and heartache to last a lifetime... unspeakable situations of cruelty, both physical and emotional, the memory of which can still bring a lump to my throat. And yet perpetrators of such raw evil have almost certainly been profoundly damaged themselves. All too often they've been on the receiving end of largely the same kinds of abuse in earlier life. Social workers are consequently faced with somehow trying to break this cycle through a myriad of measures aimed at helping improve interpersonal relationships, coping mechanisms, childcare provision, the alleviation of poverty, etc., etc.

I always felt that in a general sense happier adults made for safer children. And now, many years on, I wonder how the circumstances of some of those with whom I had been most heavily involved worked out in the fullness of time. Well, never expecting to hear from any of them ever again, you can imagine my surprise when in 2009, out of the blue, I received an email via my Facebook page. It was from a man whose adoption I had arranged all of 27 years previously when he was a little boy of five. He wanted to let me know how well things had gone since that point and to thank me for my efforts to help him. What a wonderful gesture, and although I never expected thanks for any of my social work endeavours, it's good to hear of at least one piece of work which seems to have had a happy ending.

Having spent the best part of 20 years in social work I've been left in no doubt that *'the heart of the human problem is the problem of the human heart'*. After all, if you or I had received a certain blend of genetic inheritance, behavioural conditioning and social circumstances, could *any* of us claim to be incapable of committing that which is blatantly abhorrent? Since becoming a Christian, and experiencing first hand the healing, restoring and empowering effect of the Holy Spirit in my own life, I'm convinced that only divine intervention is the real answer to the deepest of human needs.

wasn't being paid to evangelise, so I was careful never to abuse my privileged access to people's lives in this way.

Over the years this sense of frustration increased and I wondered if the Lord was loosening the ties with a view to moving me into a more overtly Christian form of employment. I applied for a number of jobs within a range of Christian organisations but was totally unsuccessful. I began to realise that the Lord would have to either move me into something else entirely or re-settle me where I was. And therefore I deliberately and decisively handed the whole thing over to Him. He would have to open a door completely as I would no longer so much as lean on one, far less try to batter it down!

COMMONWEALTH GAMES

Throughout this time I had continued to be involved in the outreach activity of Charlotte Chapel. So when Edinburgh hosted the Commonwealth Games in 1986 I was asked to represent the Chapel on an inter-church steering group that had been set up and convened by the National Bible Society of Scotland. Our remit was to explore ways in which the churches of Edinburgh could provide a Christian presence at the Games, principally in terms of outreach, hospitality and pastoral care.

WINNERS EVERYTIME

The sub-group of which I also became a member was asked to design a 'Scripture Selection', whereby a series of appropriate Bible passages would be linked together within the context of athletics. I submitted a design for this entitled 'Winners Everytime' and to my great surprise it was accepted. Around 40,000 of these were produced in full colour and went on to be used widely throughout the Games.

Now 'Winners Everytime' wasn't really what I would consider to have been an out-and-out evangelistic presentation. But through this I began to realise that there might be scope for similar publications that could explain the key concepts of the gospel in language which would be easily understandable to the man in the street.

Flushed with this unexpected 'success' it seemed a natural progression for me to explore further possibilities using an everyday theme as a basis for presenting the gospel to those who wouldn't normally consider opening a Bible or attending a church service.

  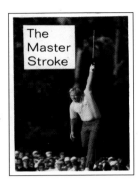

A selection of early visuals

At the time I became a Christian I felt as though I'd stumbled across a wonderful secret, and I wondered why the Church at large wasn't shouting it from the rooftops. In view of all this I set about trying to design other publications with everyday themes such as football, health, fashion etc. I was becoming increasingly convinced that there was a place for this type of literature amongst the range of outreach publications available at the time.

DESIGN AND PRESENTATION

Having worked in the printing industry for a number of years I'd developed a feel for publications that were well designed and produced. As a result I was keen to offer any ideas I had towards enhancing the standard of Christian outreach material. Yet it seemed to me that many within the Christian community at large were satisfied to see the gospel circulated in the style of yesteryear or, as was more likely, were unwilling to invest in a more contemporary form of presentation.

Of course I know that down through the years the Lord has used

SPECIFIC CONCEPTS

It seemed to me that in everyday life we're surrounded by potential visual aids which could be utilised in the furtherance of the gospel. In addition to high profile events such as the Commonwealth Games, much more mundane aspects of our daily living could also form a thematic context, such as 'shopping', 'family life', 'the environment' etc., etc. Even the towns, cities and wider geographical areas in which we live could form a basis for gospel presentations.

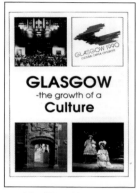

GLASGOW
-the growth of a
Culture

In my attempts to engage with prospective readers I've tried to put into practice something which was shared with me when I worked as a sales rep, long before I became a Christian. The then editor of the Church of Scotland's magazine 'Life and Work' told me that, in his opinion, the essence of true journalism is not in *telling* the reader what to believe, but rather in *leading* them to

The 'City of Culture' celebrations provided a great metaphor for the presentation of the gospel

the desired conclusion. With this in mind I've tried to write in a winsome way, confident that the Holy Spirit doesn't need my help to apply His Word to a reader's heart and mind.

It felt important for me to try to clarify a set of specific concepts that could form the philosophical foundation of - well, of course, it wasn't really anything yet - and these emerged as follows:

1. AUTHORITATIVE IN CONTENT - I wanted
to set out the essentials of the gospel, using the actual words of Scripture (the sword of the Spirit) within the context of an everyday theme. Following something of a gentle introduction I would encourage the reader to consider their personal circumstances; to recognise and 'own' their sin; to realise that in breaking God's law we all face everlasting condemnation, but that there is a way of escape. I wanted to explain the purpose and consequences of the Cross; the concept of repentance; that salvation is only through faith in the risen Christ and not by good deeds, as well as the cost of commitment.

2. ACCEPTABLE IN APPEARANCE - I wanted to develop a printed style that would have a contemporary feel and would present the gospel in an unthreatening context for the non-Christian. Something that looked too 'churchy' might result in the prospective reader never getting beyond the front cover! I also felt it important that the quality of the production and presentation should reflect something of the quality of the message.

When we think about it, literature is not independent of the form in which it's presented. In other words, on receiving a book, a leaflet or a brochure, we make immediate and largely unconscious judgements as to the value of its content. It's dangerous to judge a book by its cover - yet how easy it is to do this. So in days to come we were to pay careful attention to the design of our front covers in particular, but also the weight of the paper we would use (the heavier the paper the longer the life expectancy), the quality of colour reproduction and even the standard of folding. And in addition to all this we knew that only our best would be good enough for God who gave His best for us.

3. ADAPTABLE IN STYLE - I wanted every publication to be capable of 'customisation'. In other words, the basic designs ought to be adaptable for evangelistic use across a wide range of secular events as well as Christian organisational initiatives.

As you can see from the inside of the back cover of this book, I spent some time in clarifying Biblical principles which I felt ought to direct the design and use of any evangelistic material that would hopefully emerge in days to come. And now, almost 20 years on, I still feel that this philosophical framework has stood us in good stead, not only in day-to-day production but also as we've done what we could to advance the circulation of TELit folders.

Of course, it was one thing to have all this worked out in theory but so far nothing had been produced. Yet I kept praying and continued to look for a possible breakthrough.

Then something wonderful happened!

fellow Charlotte Chapel Elder, Donald Cameron. A very able entrepreneur, he recognised the potential of the literature I was trying to produce, especially if it could be broadened out to include secular productions. As a consequence he very kindly offered to try to create a business from it for me. This was a wonderful proposal which I found truly humbling, though I really had in mind some form of purely Christian ministry rather than a business. Donald readily accepted this point of view and, along with his wife Dorothy, has gone on to provide all kinds of very generous support and encouragement ever since.

Over the years, members of the Chapel have provided wonderful help in all kinds of ways. (As it's such a big church there seems to be an expert on just about anything!) I have never needed to purchase padded envelopes or bubble wrap, though we use these all the time. This of course doesn't just make good economic sense but good ecological sense as well. Second hand supplies are readily provided by members of the congregation, as well as advice in respect of every facet of TELit's functioning. Not only does this help us financially, it's true Christian fellowship in action and bears testimony to the fact that TELit is a real collaborative effort.

A REAL DILEMMA

At this point I was faced with the question of what to call the type of publication I was trying to develop. As the 1980's drew to a close I felt I ought to settle on some term or other that would best describe the type of publication that seemed to be emerging.

Now, most of my Christian friends referred to these as 'tracts', as indeed do many of our clients right up to the present day. However, I would have to admit I'm not a great fan of this term when used to describe our product, for three basic reasons:

   1. The word 'tract' for me brings with it some unhelpful connotations of yesteryear and is not an accurate description of what TELit has aimed to produce from day one. For example, the term 'tract' can conjure up the impression of a Christian leaflet, invariably produced on low quality paper, with little colour, few pictures and in very small print. I have

the greatest respect for those who wrote and produced such evangelistic literature in days gone by and multitudes of Christians have been able to trace their conversion to the reading of a tract. But my conviction is that, to a very large extent, the day of this type of publication is now over.

2. I also dislike the term because all too often I've heard it follow three particular words -'It's only a ...!' and in view of this I'd be concerned in case the gospel may be cheapened or trivialised. The design and production of every Christian publication ought to reflect the quality of the message it's seeking to communicate and thus commend it to the reader. Therefore it's essential that we avoid anything which might undermine its perceived value.

3. The third reason is one of economics. In days gone by tracts were produced in large quantities at very low cost. Unfortunately much of this mindset has been carried forward by Christians into the modern day. As a result, TELit found it extremely difficult to charge a realistic price for the type of literature we were producing, especially in the early years.

So, what should we call our style of publication? Well, it had the flexibility and general appeal of a tract produced in a contemporary format but it contained a significant number of Bible references, more in keeping with a Scripture Selection (where a number of Bible verses are arranged in accordance with a particular theme). I therefore decided to call our product an 'evangelistic folder'. Though not too snappy perhaps, it's an accurate and understandable expression for today's society. Yet from the very beginning I realised that whatever we actually

It doesn't matter what our publications are called, so long as they're made available - here on a wall in Cambridge

called our product would really be of little consequence in the final analysis. The real challenge was the extent to which Christians would actually want to use our material in personal and corporate outreach. The following article from 'Evangelism

would I have found the time to do all the necessary organisation and administration? However, the Lord appears to have seen things rather differently and I was soon to have some spare time which I didn't anticipate!

GOD OF THE UNEXPECTED

Now, as it happened, in 1988 I underwent a minor medical procedure on an out-patient basis. I'd been told to take things easy for the remainder of that particular day, but in the evening I attended an important Elders' Meeting at the Chapel. This was not a sensible move however as I began to experience considerable pain and had to leave early. This got worse throughout the night and by the next day I had been admitted to Edinburgh Royal Infirmary in agony. I was told that my failure to rest the previous evening had brought about internal bleeding.

Following my discharge from hospital I was prescribed total bed rest for three weeks. In fact I didn't have much choice in this as it was impossible for me to stand upright, such was the intensity of the pain. But I managed to prop myself up in bed with my mother's old portable typewriter on my lap and set about using the time as profitably as possible.

During this period I did a lot of serious thinking and praying. And in due course I was to see something of a breakthrough in terms of the way ahead. Looking back I have no doubt that my enforced incapacity was ordained by the Lord. After all, how else would I have had a chunk of time made available to me through which such foundational progress could take place - despite my physical limitations.

I have no doubt that these weeks, during which I was to suffer excruciating pain, formed a milestone in the history of TELit. Although formal establishment as a charitable trust was still a year or so away, I look back on this period as having being crucial in determining the future of the work. And perhaps the fact that this time was characterised by pain is not without significance. After all, so much of the spread of Christianity and the growth of the Church has been achieved through pain, sacrifice and even apparent failure. Yes, God certainly does move in some pretty mysterious ways His wonders to perform.

A NAME, A DESCRIPTION AND A CHALLENGE

I knew that the work needed to be called something, though I've never wanted my name to be used in this context, especially as it's never been *my* work. I wanted it to be something memorable, engaging and with a contemporary ring. After a while it dawned on me that as I was hoping to produce 'thematic evangelistic literature' I could construct from this term the acronym TELit. And the fact that such a name would also have a double meaning seemed to me to be a wonderful bonus, though it soon became clear that the significance of the spelling of TELit was lost on many of those who would have dealings with us. But

THEMATIC EVANGELISTIC LITERATURE

8 NOBLE PLACE, EDINBURGH EH6 8AX   TELEPHONE: 031-554 0339

My first homemade attempt at a letterheading!

just as I've grown used to the many, varied versions I receive regarding my own surname, so I've become equally accustomed to the variety of ways in which TELit is spelt. After all, the bottom line for me is that if someone wants to use our publications to help others seek the Lord then they can spell it absolutely any way they like!

Now that I had hit on a name I set about putting together a logo that could be used in all future publications and would help form our corporate image.

By the dawn of 1989 I felt that some real progress was being made. And yet I knew that it was necessary to see some form of organisational and administrative structure put in place. With this in mind, and in prayerful consultation with friends in Charlotte Chapel, things were set to take another step forward.

Therefore, I adopted a very simple strategy when looking for new Trustees. Maureen and I would ask the Lord to make clear who His choice would be. And as a result someone has always emerged who seemed to have a real heart for the work and with whom I could enjoy excellent spiritual rapport.

I'm sure that every organisation is really only as good as its people. And with this in mind it's been a real privilege over the years to lead the work of TELit alongside so many quality Trustees and Directors. Our pattern has been to hold three or four Trustee meetings per year, usually in our home, and although Maureen and I were original Trustees, we relinquished this responsibility when I became an employee of TELit. As I see it, the main focus of the Trustees' involvement is to discern the way ahead. But in addition to their collective contribution we've also benefited considerably from the specific knowledge and skills of particular individuals, especially in terms of finance and technology.

We've also enjoyed a harmony and unity which I'm sure would be the envy of many an organisation. Though each has brought their own unique personality and outlook to bear upon the work, their united commitment to the furtherance of the gospel has proved a wonderful basis for progress and development. I would have to acknowledge however that whilst I've always been able to rely on the support of each successive chairman and have welcomed their ideas, none has ever 'interfered' with the designing of the material or the day-to-day running of the Trust. I'm sure that this 'hands off' approach has contributed significantly to the level of production which has been achieved over the past 20 years. After all, if Noah had been a committee, the Ark might never have been built!

TRUSTEES and DIRECTORS

TELit owes a tremendous debt of gratitude to the following men and women who have given many hours of considerable effort in order to help see the work progress.

The TELit Trust: January 1990 - June 2004

Trustees

Paul Cocking	1990-1993	Chairman 1990-1993
George Harley	1990-1992	
Maureen Sprott	1990-1997	
	2000-2004	
John Grant	1990-1993	
Donald Cameron	1990-2000	Chairman 1994-2000
Barry Sprott	1990-1994	
Dave Sharpe	1992-2004	Chairman 2000-2004
Dorothy Bartlett	1992-1995	
Angie Speer	1994-1998	
Jeremy Landless	1994-1996	
Mary Harrison	1995-2004	
Sam Barron	1996-2004	
Judy White	1997-2004	Chairman 2004
Mervyn Barter	2000-2004	
Gordon Lindhorst	2003-2004	

The Thematic Evangelistic Literature Company Limited: July 2004 - now

Directors

Judy White	2004-2008	Chairman 2004-2008
Barry Sprott	2004-2006	
Mary Harrison	2004-now	
Gordon Lindhorst	2004-now	Chairman 2008-now
Mervyn Barter	2004-2005	
James Deans	2004-now	
Maureen Sprott	2004-2006	
Sam Barron	2004-2004	
Donald Bain	2006-now	
Diane Falconer	2008-now	

continues to order TELit folders on a regular basis. Praise the Lord!

Over the next few years we hired a stand at a number of Christian Resources Exhibitions in different parts of the country. During the course of one of these in 1994, in Manchester, I remember a particular encouragement. A man approached our stand and glancing at the display of evangelistic literature said, *'Whatever you do, don't give up. I became a Christian through this kind of thing.'* He then disappeared into the crowd.

In addition to these major events I also managed to have a presence at the likes of the Fellowship of Independent Evangelical Churches Convention in Caister, the Scottish Baptist Youth Assembly and even the Buckie Keswick! In fact, I would go anywhere if it would put me into conversation with prospective clients of TELit.

Of course this kind of publicity is not always cost-efficient and I've always found it difficult to know how best to use the Lord's resources. This dilemma is well explained through the following:

'However much we would like advertising to be a science - because life would be simpler that way - the fact is that it is not. It is a subtle, ever-changing art, defying formulisation, flowering on freshness and withering on imitation; where what was effective one day, for that very reason, will not be effective the next, because it has lost the maximum impact of originality.'

Bill Bernbach

TEL**it**

THEMATIC EVANGELISTIC LITERATURE

●

*Heralding a new generation of outreach literature for personal and corporate evangelism.

*Providing a thematic presentation for all kinds of Christian and secular events.

*Offering a custom - design facility for a wide variety of settings and activities.

●

Thematic Evangelistic Literature

8 Noble Place, EDINBURGH EH6 8AX

Telephone: 031-554 0339

Early publicity leaflet used at exhibitions

DIRECT MAIL

Marketing professionals have known for years that product recommendation from a trusted friend is among the most effective means of advertising and it's also the least expensive (you can tell I'm a true Scotsman!). But in these early days most people had never even heard of TELit. I was sure that our best advert was our finished product and therefore it was necessary to discover ways by which we could get sample titles into the possession of decision-makers in churches and Christian organisations.

Now at this stage TELit didn't have a computer, nor did many churches have their own website. Therefore, on a number of occasions we purchased a selected range of names and addresses on self-adhesive labels and used these to post relevant TELit information to church leaders. On reflection, and although it is very difficult to measure the success of such an initiative, I doubt if this was a particularly cost-effective exercise. Nevertheless, just as George Verwer of Operation Mobilisation - a great long-term encourager of TELit - considers everyone to be either a *'missionary'* or a *'mission field'*, so every TELit folder is valuable in one way or another. After all, every single copy falling into someone's hands has the capacity to either encourage them as a believer or challenge them in such a way that they might be brought to saving faith. So, although direct mail might not have appeared to have been particularly fruitful in generating prospective clients, who knows what the Lord has done in the lives of all who received and read these samples. In fact, I have never considered the sending out of a TELit folder to have been wasted, in view of His promise:

> *'As the rain and snow come down from heaven, and do not return to it without watering the earth and making it bud and flourish, so that it yields seed for the sower and bread for the eater, so is my word that goes out from my mouth: It will not return to me empty, but will accomplish what I desire and achieve the purpose for which I sent it.'*
>
> **Isaiah 55:10-11**

In light of this, I have always wanted to encourage the liberal use of our material as it's vitally important that we communicate the gospel to as many as possible. This seems so important to me in our increasingly secular society. After all, who knows which particular copies will prove most fruitful. And as my former pastor Rev Derek Prime once reminded me, in the parable of the sower there was no rebuke for the liberality with which the seed was sown, despite only a proportion having borne fruit.

An early TELit advert

THE CHRISTIAN PRESS

If direct mail proved to have been only moderately effective, then the Christian press was even less so. Back in these early years I was very naive. I was sure that just as I was full of enthusiasm for what was a totally new concept in literature evangelism, so the editors of Christian periodicals would be falling over themselves to make TELit known to the great British Christian public. But how wrong could I be! By and large their responses to my overtures were underwhelming in the extreme. I couldn't understand why many magazines were so resistant to my requests that they feature the emergence of TELit. Apart from a tiny minority they just didn't want to know and seemed interested only in trying to sell us advertising space. We did purchase some in these early years but because of the costs involved and what we considered to be a very poor return, we didn't think it was a wise use of the resources the Lord was giving us. We soon abandoned this method of publicity. After all, most prospective clients want to read and handle the product rather than just see a small picture of a front cover!

WORD OF MOUTH

From day one my long term personal objective has been to become a world class Christian, though I know I have a long way to go. With a similar outlook I've always wanted TELit to become a world class ministry - not in terms of public prominence, nor in any other ways the world could measure us - but in the eyes of the Lord. With this in mind I've always felt it vitally important that He Himself should determine the pace of our growth, as well as setting our day-to-day agenda. My priority was to see TELit develop in significance rather than in size, though the two are not necessarily mutually exclusive.

It was always a great joy to return home from work each evening to discover we'd received an enquiry, or even an order. Most times I had no idea how a particular person had heard of us but was simply grateful to know that someone or something had pointed them in our direction. Over the years, word of mouth has indeed proved the best form of advertising.

Many, many people have contributed to the growth of TELit in this way, but perhaps none more so than Robin Fairbairn, who for a number of years was Assistant Secretary with Belfast City Mission. He became a great enthusiast for TELit material and

A tiny selection of titles for N. Ireland all
beginning with the letter 'B'!

as he preached Sunday by Sunday throughout the Province he rarely failed to fly the flag for the work wherever he went. This resulted in our receiving requests for the design and production of evangelistic folders featuring dozens of places in Northern

Ireland. In fact, we've done so many of these over the years that our one-time Northern Irish Trustee, Sam Barron, remarked that instead of swapping pictures of footballers in the playgrounds of Ulster the youngsters probably exchange TELit folders! When we went on to produce children's material, Robin enthusiastically used this to design his own sketch-board presentations for school assemblies. But Belfast City Mission helped us in many other ways, even allowing us to share

Sharing a Belfast City Mission exhibition stand at a Christian Resources Exhibition

a display stand at Christian Resources Exhibitions. The cost of exhibiting at these events can run into many hundreds of pounds and therefore such wonderful gestures of practical partnership in the gospel have meant so much over the years.

TELit truly owes a great deal to Belfast City Mission. Under the leadership of George Ferguson, they used hundreds of thousands of TELit folders, and even provided accommodation for us to form a sub-office in the city. I will always be profoundly grateful to George, Robin and their colleagues, godly men with whom I've shared many an hour in precious fellowship.

The Lord has also helped make the work more widely known through friends who have left Edinburgh. As a result of Kenny and Margaret Armstrong moving to Doncaster; Steve and Anne Hailes to Leighton Buzzard, and Iain and Linda Campbell to Bangor, Co.Down, more churches began using TELit material.

Through all of this the work grew steadily and firmly, despite many set-backs along the way. In these early days I often felt frustrated that the work was not expanding faster. But on reflection I realise that had the pace of progress been more dramatic I would have struggled to cope. The Lord was determining our rate of growth, graciously taking into account our capacities and limitations. And every day He seemed to reassure us with fresh evidences of His gracious love and care.

Chapter 13

Money Matters

'...when you give to the needy, do not announce it with trumpets...'

Matthew 6:2

When TELit was established in 1990 I wanted it to take the form of a ministry rather than a business. That's not to say of course that it shouldn't be run along standard business lines; rather, I didn't want it to become predominantly a commercial enterprise. In fact, if TELit could function without money altogether then I would have been more than happy! But of course the harsh realities of life dictate otherwise and I realised from the start that the more that was received, the more that could be achieved.

GENERAL PRINCIPLE

As a young Christian my attitude to money had been greatly influenced by Maureen's parents. They were career missionaries serving initially as church planters in Ghana with WEC (Worldwide Evangelisation Crusade) and latterly with the Leprosy Mission in Thailand. They never made

Alan & Charlese Davis

their financial needs known to anyone other than the Lord and as a consequence found that such needs were always met. Over many years they had the thrill of seeing wonderful answers to prayer and as they themselves were extremely generous, they proved that the Lord is no man's debtor. I decided to follow their example and this became the general principle which underpinned the financial affairs of TELit.

Adopting the philosophy of Hudson Taylor, founder of the China Inland Mission, now OMF (Overseas Missionary Fellowship) -

66

arithmetic at Night School!). One of the basic problems with this was that some folders were much more expensive to produce than others for various reasons. Setting a standard price for all titles appeared a more manageable option, especially as such arrangements could become so complex. And of course time was not on my side. In those days I was working full-time in my secular employment and trying to keep a whole number of other plates spinning at the same time. So what should we do?

Option 4 Charge what the marketplace accepts

After considering all the various options, the bottom line had to be whether or not the purchasing public would buy the product! We could have fixed the price at what we felt was a fair level for what the purchaser would get for their money, but in this particular sphere it wasn't as simple as that. We had to be guided by our 'competitors' in this (I prefer the term 'complementary ministries'). And although I was convinced that our product was of a higher quality in a number of ways to that being produced by some other publishers, would this be recognised and accepted by decision-makers in churches and Christian organisations?

Sadly I was soon to discover that to many, literature evangelism was becoming an optional expense rather than an essential investment. And all too often there would be a sharp intake of breath when I informed a telephone enquirer that the basic price per folder had been fixed at 10p per copy, with discounts on bulk quantities. *'But it's only a tract'*, they would go on to say, *'I can get the same thing for half the price elsewhere!'* Well, this is one of the reasons we don't call our publications 'tracts' (see Chapter 9). I would also seriously doubt if 'the same thing' *would* be available elsewhere! Our materials and design are invariably of a different quality to many 'tracts' still being produced today.

However, taking everything into consideration, we stuck with the price of 10p per copy throughout these early years and the Lord saw to it that we were able to muddle along quite successfully.

FINANCIAL SUPPORT

From the very outset of the work I was aware of various business 'start up' sources of funding, which were available both locally and nationally. However, I felt it would be better to forgo these opportunities and instead rely solely upon the Lord for finance.

Money can be a wonderful servant but a dreadful master, and a number of organisations have run aground through their 'mishandling' of financial resources. Well aware of many potential pitfalls in this sphere, we've always considered every penny that came our way to have come from the Lord, and as such was His provision for the work. This gave us the incentive to exercise the best of stewardship, though perhaps my earlier association with future Chancellor, Gordon Brown, also helped me exercise prudence in such matters!

So from the very beginning we began asking the Lord for what we felt we needed and there's no doubt that He prompted particular people to provide financial support. Over the years this has been forthcoming in a number of unpredictable ways. For example, on one occasion Maureen and I met a young couple who were new to the Chapel and invited them to lunch. Although TELit was mentioned in the course of conversation that day, no reference was made to our financial needs. Therefore, it came as an enormous surprise when, within the next week or so, there arrived the largest single gift that TELit has ever received.

Once the Trust was established, a small group of supporters began to emerge. To begin with these were largely from within our network of family and close friends, although this was to broaden out in years to come.

I produced an explanatory leaflet entitled 'Introducing TELit' as a way of setting out our aims and objectives, and this proved helpful in generating interest and financial support. By this time my mother's old typewriter had bitten the dust and Maureen and I decided to invest in an Amstrad computer (remember them?). Thankfully I had taught myself to type, largely through producing regular Prayer Letters for my sister Lenna and her husband Julyan, who for fifteen years served with Operation Mobilisation in Turkey. I was now much more productive and wrote to many Christian organisations, not for funds, but in the hope of stimulating interest in what we were trying to do.

An important decision to be made fairly early on was whether or not to ask clients for payment in advance of supplying their order. This practice was being adopted by an increasing number of organisations similar to our own. But we decided against following their example.

Although it may seem rather naive of me I felt that prepayment should not be necessary as Christians by and large would be trustworthy. And secondly, I would be afraid that in the time it might take for a church leader to organise payment from their Treasurer, enthusiasm to use the material might dissipate! Therefore, I would rather strike while the iron was hot and get the folders into the hands of those who wanted to use them. The paperwork could follow thereafter.

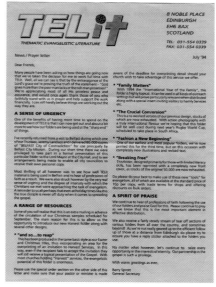

An early newsletter

On reflection, this arrangement has worked very well, although I'm sorry to say that too often for my liking we've had to chase overdue accounts. I try to do this as gently as I can as it would be all too easy to cause upset or offence, especially in situations of bereavement or honest human frailty. Sadly we've had to write off a number of bad debts over the years, but then TELit has always been a fairly risky business.

One thing that disappoints me even more however is the growing practice of clients haggling over price. I realise that those who use large quantities of literature on a regular basis need to be able to expect significant discount arrangements and we always do our very best in this respect. Yet so often it seems to me, here is another example of worldly values finding their way into the Church. There have actually been occasions when in response to haggling I've given quantities of folders away free of charge knowing that my God is big enough to see that we don't lose out as a result of this.

Nevertheless, there have also been times when an impoverished Christian Union or the like has approached us requesting help to enable them to respond to some upcoming outreach opportunity. In such circumstances we've had no hesitation in providing a gift of literature. And our experience has usually been that within the next week or so someone totally unconnected with the request has sent us a cheque, often for more than the value of whatever had been given away! Our policy has been never to allow finance alone prevent someone using our material. Over the years we've increased our basic folder price only twice - from 10p to 12p in 1995 and from 12p to 15p in 1997. We've always wanted to absorb cost increases as best we could in the hope of ensuring that our prices were never pitched beyond the financial reach of even the smallest Fellowship. But the cost of paper

'Knowing the Way' was designed specifically for outreach to students and has so far been produced in 3 separate editions

and colour printing has always been one of our most challenging overheads.

PRINTING AND PRINTERS

From the very outset I've considered myself to be TELit's back stop; the bottom line; the person who will, in the final analysis, be accountable for every facet of the work. And of course it's always been incumbent upon me to exercise responsibility in the use of the Lord's money. With this in mind, the experience and understanding I gained in my eight years in the printing industry

74

have proved much more valuable than I could have imagined. Although much of the technology has changed dramatically, some of the basic principles of the printing process haven't.

Over the years we've used many printers both in the UK and overseas and have built up not only good working relationships with key personnel, but also enduring friendships. We've been particularly grateful for all the help provided by the likes of Andrew Sehne of Wright's (Printers) Ltd in Sandbach; Chris and Cathy Powell of CPO Ltd in Worthing; Chris Wallis of Print by Design Ltd in Bodmin; Jim and Jackie Cree of City Litho Ltd in Edinburgh, and Jim McClean who has organised much of our production in Northern Ireland.

Printing is a highly competitive industry. Over-capacity, especially in times of recession, has forced many firms to the wall and as the work has grown we've been approached by a steady stream of companies anxious to print our literature. After all, given that we do all the origination ourselves and that our print runs are usually quite substantial... well I would love to have come across TELit in the days when I was a sales rep! But in this, as in every aspect of the work, we've looked to the Lord and as a result I feel that for the most part, we've used the right companies at the right times for particular types of work.

RECEIVING - A SPIRITUAL DISCIPLINE

From the very beginning the functioning of TELit has never been self-financing in a commercial sense and has been subsidised through the giving of God's people. It's no exaggeration to say that irrespective of how hard I've worked over these years the survival of TELit and indeed the Sprott family has been dependent, to a large extent, upon financial gifts.

But I must admit to having found this very difficult to accept, especially in the early years, as this practical reality stood in marked contrast to some of my attitudes, values and natural instincts. I have a strong work ethic and am very grateful never to have had a day's unemployment from the day I started my first job on leaving school in 1966. Since becoming a Christian I've also been a firm believer in God's order for the family as set out in Scripture. He makes it clear that, as head of a household, the man's role ought to be that of leader, defender and provider on behalf of his dependants. Therefore my responsibility as provider gave me a good deal of moral perplexity when I entered full-time employment with TELit.

Yet in time I began to appreciate that in Christian ministry a gift of money must never be perceived as a form of hand-out. In fact, reluctance to accept such a gift is likely to result in the spiritual (and perhaps even the financial) impoverishment of the giver. The truth underlying this apparent paradox is confirmed by the Lord Jesus Christ telling us that it's more blessed to give that to receive. And we've proved from experience that He can never be outdone in giving.

I've developed an attitude of gratitude over the years and yet, as a proportion of the gifts we receive have always been anonymous, it's been impossible to thank anyone for these, other than the Lord. One such example concerned the approach of our 25th Wedding Anniversary when we hoped we could visit a dear friend who was studying at Bible College in Canada. You can imagine our shock when we returned from an evening service to find a plain brown envelope containing £900 in £10 notes having been stuffed through our letterbox. Yes, the Lord knows all of our needs and can prompt His people accordingly.

It's so important for Christian Trusts to be 'whiter than white' and for there to be absolutely no suggestion of financial or, for that matter, any other form of impropriety. For this reason we've never administered payroll arrangements ourselves, always preferring this to be organised at 'arms length' through independent accounting arrangements. Over the years we've been indebted to those who have looked after our finances, namely George Harley, Nelson Yui, Dave Sharpe, Mary Harrison, Dorothy Bartlett, Denise Cranston, Mervyn Barter and Gordon Menzies. Each has been a real God-send and none more so than our current book-keeper, Mary Hume, for whom nothing is too much trouble. Mary came along at just the right time and has been such a blessing to us in so many ways.

Chapter 14

Planning the Way Ahead

*'Unless the LORD builds the house,
its builders labour in vain.'*

Psalm 127:1

It's been my aim from the very beginning to produce evangelistic literature that would present the essence of the Christian gospel faithfully and do so in a manner that would honour the Lord. To have seen the work grow and develop in many different ways over the years has been a great thrill and yet I've always known that the Lord could bring it all to an end overnight should He so wish. Therefore first and foremost I had to be convinced that things were moving in accordance with His will and purposes.

I remember on one occasion, very early on, asking the Lord to give me some form of sign that the work had His approval and He did so in a most unusual way.

GOD OF THE UNEXPECTED

Back in 1991 we produced one of our very first titles for a particular place. 'Kilmarnock and You' was commissioned by a Brethren Assembly who planned to get a copy into every home in the town. Not long after this had been printed, there was one occasion on which I returned from work whilst Maureen, along with the girls, was on a trip to Thailand. At that stage in my life I hadn't yet become a 'new man' so, well aware of my culinary limitations, I nipped round the corner to our local chip shop for a fish supper. To save having to wash a plate (typical man) I began eating straight from the paper whilst watching the news. Suddenly a heading on the newspaper in which it was wrapped caught my eye. It referred to Christians in Kilmarnock having commissioned an Edinburgh company to produce what they called a piece of 'publicity material' for distribution throughout the town. I couldn't believe what I was reading and wondered how an Edinburgh newspaper had heard of this project. But when I read the name at the corner of the page I discovered it was the *Kilmarnock Standard*!

I would have been amazed to read something about TELit in *any* newspaper but then the likelihood of all this actually happening in the way it had started to dawn on me. I began to appreciate just how much of a sign from heaven this most probably was. When I considered the number of chip shops in Edinburgh, the piles of newspapers in all of these, the likelihood of a Kilmarnock paper being amongst them, the chances of the article in question being on the page which wrapped my fish supper etc., etc. Well, this was certainly a big enough sign convincing me that the Lord was indeed in the work.

But in addition to this, and well after the 'Kilmarnock' folder had been distributed throughout the town, we received some very positive feedback from those who had initiated the venture. By the following year over 70 responses had been received and a number of these people had gone on to form significant relationships with the church in question.

Amongst those seeking more information were four young Mormon missionaries; a taxi driver who became so intrigued with the Scripture content he borrowed a Bible from the local library; two students studying comparative religions, and a man with a history of self-abuse for which this formed some kind of lifeline.

ANOTHER UNEXPECTED 'SIGN'

Also in 1990 another very unusual event occurred that seemed to reinforce the conviction I already had that the Lord was working in and through TELit.

An opportunity had arisen for me to display our publications at the *FIEC Convention at Caister, near Great Yarmouth. In the

* Fellowship of International Evangelical Churches

course of this event I was standing in the queue for lunch when a man behind me struck up a conversation. We spoke about our respective churches and he told me that his was in extremely good heart. They had been participating recently in an Operation Mobilisation outreach initiative within the city of Leicester and had been particularly encouraged by the level of responses received. He then went on to say that he considered the most positive feature of the whole thing to have been a specially produced piece of literature through which the message of the gospel had been set within the context of Leicester. When he discovered that I had written it and

CHANGE
in
LEICESTER

had produced 25,000 copies of these for this venture, I'm not sure which of us was more amazed at this 'coincidence'! But for me this was yet another very encouraging sign from on high.

THE CRITICAL TIME FACTOR

Before I became a Christian I would have to admit that my life was loosely patterned on the idea that when God made time

How I looked in the early 70's!

he made plenty of it! Dressed in my lavender denim suit, I liked nothing better than dancing and romancing the night away in the discos of Fife, and now, looking back, I wonder how I managed to hold down my job as a sales rep. I was often driving 100 miles a day and probably it was only by God's grace that I never fell asleep at the wheel. Saturday nights were such an important time for me that it was common practice for me to sleep throughout much of the following day! But when I came to know the Lord on 26th April '74 things changed virtually overnight. Instead of being a 'nothing' day, Sunday became the best and most important day of the week. And I was given a new appreciation of the value of

79

time. As I reflected upon all that the Lord had done for me on the Cross of Calvary I wanted my life to really count for Him. If Christians are His hands and feet in this world then I wanted my life to make a real difference for the eternal benefit of others and as an expression of my gratitude to Him.

As I began to mature spiritually I became aware of His changing me gradually from an owl to a lark. And of course many years into the future I was to find this absolutely essential in the interests of TELit.

As the work began to take off, time became my greatest challenge. How could I keep so many plates spinning at the one time? My full time employment involved providing and overseeing social work services to adolescents throughout one of the largest sectors of the city - Wester Hailes, Gorgie/Dalry and rapidly becoming notorious for the prevalence of drug abuse - Muirhouse. I was serving as an Elder in my church and had a wife and young family. I also had a wide circle of good friends with whom to keep contact. And these were only the *major* areas of responsibility I had. Where and how could TELit fit into all of this?

I realised however that it is not God who overworks us, it's usually ourselves, and therefore I *did* have sufficient opportunity to do the things that really mattered, so long as I disciplined myself in my use of time. So I began to develop the habit of rising at around 6.00am each week day - a practice I still follow today - and doing an hour or so of TELit work before leaving for my office in the Social Work Department. Lunch breaks were also invariably given over to designing some folder or other, although I did my best not to bring work home as I wanted to protect quality family time. I'm still reluctant to do any TELit work at home if I can help it and still rise early, probably for three important reasons. Firstly, following my conversion I've wanted to redeem the fruitless years which had been given over largely to carnal pursuits! Secondly, I've tried to take on board some of the insights outlined in Gordon MacDonald's excellent book *Ordering your Private World*. In this he encourages readers to better understand and utilise their natural intellectual abilities and capacities. For me the most productive time is early morning as my sharpness seems to tail off progressively during the day.

Thirdly, I try to follow the exhortations of 18th century Puritan, Jonathan Edwards, 'to spend and be spent for Him', and then at the end of each day, 'to lie down under His smiles'.

The Lord had given us three lovely daughters, Joanna, Rachel and Rebekah, and although I would have liked to have had a son to whom I would have introduced the joys of football, this was not to be. But then of course I have only myself to blame for this as biologically I determined the sex of my children anyway! However in the providence of God this has all worked out for the best. Although I've always enjoyed a very warm relationship with all three, being girls they've gravitated more naturally over the years to their mother than to their father. (When they were younger they would never have wanted me take them shopping for clothes!) This meant I was spared the time that I would otherwise have wanted to spend with a boy. But how should I try to make best use of this most precious commodity for TELit?

WHICH FOLDERS SHOULD I WORK ON?

I wanted my 'TELit time' to be as productive as it could be, and therefore I wondered if there would be some way of determining which opportunities to pursue. As the work became more well

An example of a folder produced for a youth organisation but which never materialised into print

known I began to receive requests for specific designs and,

carried away with energy and enthusiasm, I felt I had to respond as positively as I could to each one. I also produced designs on a purely speculative basis in the hope that something might happen to see them into print. I have to admit that the net result is a fairly large box containing many 'themes' that have been developed to the artwork stage but have never been printed, e.g. 'United We Stand' on the subject of Trade Unionism.

Written back in 1990 but reprinted many times since then

But as the years went by I became far more discriminating. The problem was, I could be approached by someone who seemed to be prepared to run with a particular project or other, yet after my origination work had been done there was a change of direction at their end and the endeavour was largely wasted. I'm sorry to say that it's not the first time a church leader has commissioned some work or other only to then fall out with his colleagues and for the church to be reluctant to honour the commitment he had made. Nevertheless, the Lord has always seen us through such circumstances and these are the exceptions to the rule. Working within a Christian business environment the vast majority of clients are of course very honourable people.

Nowadays in trying to decide which title or other to develop I have a far better idea as to the respective commercial viability of prospective products, although I've found this to be more an art than a science. It's very difficult to discern the Lord's guidance in such matters but as a rough rule of thumb I now usually won't progress any new general title until at least three people have suggested this to me independently of one another.

DESIGNING A FOLDER

I'm often asked how I go about putting a new design together, and although the technology at my disposal today is far superior to what was available to me at the beginning, my basic approach hasn't really changed.

First of all I badly need some peace and quiet. I've tried to write text when others are around and I can spend half an hour trying to get an introduction right. I just can't do it. I'm simply too easily distracted. The best time of day for me to write is the early morning. However, this hasn't always been possible and a number of titles, such as 'Titanic', 'The Right Route' and 'Family Matters', were written in bed. Although I trusted the Lord for inspiration, He expected me to provide the perspiration and I really just had to seize opportunities when they came along. For example, 'The Crucial Conversion' was written in my car waiting for the ferry to take me from Larne to Stranraer. But in more recent years almost all folders have been written between 7.30am and 9.30am in the TELit office.

I always begin in the same way, with prayer. I commit the whole thing to the Lord and say virtually, *'Where do I go from here?'* But although I have a blank piece of paper in front of me I also have a theological template in my head. In other words, no matter what the theme may be, a place, an event, a sport or some general aspect of life, there's always the same irreducible minimum of spiritual ground I feel I need to cover.

As I'm trying to present an overview of the main concepts inherent in the gospel the big challenge facing me is how I can link specific features of the subject in question to these concepts, without the links appearing too contrived. I'm always trying to explain the unfamiliar through the familiar and my overriding concern is that the Lord will speak through the Scripture verses, the key element in each publication.

I write everything out long hand, but at times the words seem to come to me so quickly that I'm racing to write them down. Just as in *Chariots of Fire* Eric Liddell claims to feel God's pleasure when he runs, I can experience something similar as I write. I'm also asked how big a part the computer plays in the design process yet I'd have to admit that at the origination stage, it's none!

Recent years have seen quite a lot of arthritic pain develop in my right hand, but above my desk I have a little picture on the wall which helps keep things in perspective for me. It's an image of a crown of thorns together with the words 'Love hurts'.

I also consider it a great privilege to be handling Scripture as much as I do. In fact, although I'm usually dealing with pretty much the same verses, the truth behind them comes to me on occasion with fresh clarity and impetus as well as renewed appreciation. At such times I struggle to keep writing as my eyes will have filled with tears. It's just as well I'm on my own as I'd be a bit embarrassed otherwise.

Example of one of our earliest 'thumbnails'

While I'm in the throes of putting a new folder together like this I often like to pause and visualise some of our supporters at their work or other day-to-day activities. This helps me remember that TELit is truly a team effort and that I'm writing as much on their behalf as my own.

Once the text is written and I've decided where the graphics should go, I then draw up a 'thumbnail' of the whole thing ready for a colleague to assemble on computer. In days gone by we had to put all of this together in large sheets of artwork ready for colour separation prior to platemaking and printing, but our in-house technology now makes life much more straightforward in this respect.

Once completed, computer printouts are produced ready to be assembled into a colour visual for consideration by the client. After approval the whole thing can be emailed or saved onto CD and sent to one of our printers for production.

In all honesty I'd have to say that I'm very rarely entirely happy with the finished product. Setting aside the various printing or folding glitches which arise from time to time, I'm usually less than content with what I've written. I rarely feel I've produced anything other than a pretty clumsy attempt at expressing in summary what is beyond the shadow of a doubt the greatest story ever told.

DISTRIBUTION ARRANGEMENTS

Another important decision to be made as orders began to come in was how we could best transport our publications to our clients. Specific commissions could often be sent directly from the printer but other orders were not so simple. At this stage in our development we just weren't geared up to despatching items as they needed to be. Literature can so easily become damaged in transit so we began to look elsewhere for help. We entered into discussions with the wholesale section of CLC (Christian Literature Crusade) in Hampshire to explore the possibility of their becoming distribution agents for us. However financial constraints rendered this option a non-starter. Instead I decided to make up the parcels myself and got to know my local sub-postmaster very well!

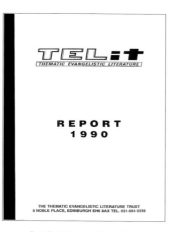

Our first Annual Report

TAKING STOCK

By the end of 1990 we had produced and circulated almost 200,000 folders in 13 titles. I felt very encouraged by the steady growth of the work and put together a form of Annual Report. This was to summarise what had been achieved but also to help clarify the way ahead.

Although we had no venture capital we were keeping our heads above water and had much for which to be grateful to both our small band of supporters and the Lord. Nevertheless I was, and am still to this day, a bit disappointed by the degree to which churches and Christian organisations are reluctant to put serious money into evangelistic literature. After all, millions are spent each year on buildings so we can all worship more comfortably the God who 'does not live in temples built by hands' (Acts 17:24). This is how I expressed such a view in our first Report:

> *'As a general observation however, it does concern and disappoint me to compare the level of resources provided for the comfort, interest and 'maintenance' of those of us already in the Kingdom, as opposed to that which is made available for reaching the multitudes out there, bound for a lost eternity.'*

I readily admit to having a very biased view on such matters. But when I consider the life-changing and destiny-securing power of the gospel then I feel we ought to be prepared to crawl over broken glass to get this message to those who appear oblivious to the peril they face.

Our first attempt at presenting
the gospel through
'The Beautiful Game'

It was reported in Patrick Johnstone's *Operation World* that more than half of all evangelical Christians attribute their conversion, at least in part, to Christian literature. But, according to *Tear Times* back in 1975, 90% of all Christian literature is produced for a Christian audience. In view of this, I committed myself to do all I could to redress the balance!

And yet on a much more practical and perhaps mundane level we also finished the year wondering how we could find more space for storage as this was becoming a pressing problem.

Chapter 15

The Working Environment

'My heart is stirred by a noble theme...'

Psalm 45:1

I received a letter one day from a man who drew my attention to this particular verse of Scripture. He considered it quite intriguing and perhaps significant that I was engaged in producing *thematic* evangelistic literature from 8 *Noble* Place!

This had been our home for the preceding ten years or so, an Edinburgh colony style upper villa flat not far from Leith Links. We were situated towards the far end of Noble Place which was a cul-de-sac. The street was therefore an extension of our tiny garden for the children, who spent many happy hours there playing with their friends. Accommodation indoors was tight and there was simply nowhere to properly establish the expanding work of TELit.

Rachel happily trusting Joanna for a ride down Noble Place under the watchful eye of Mum

But some very significant developments were soon to take place.

RESTRUCTURING... FOR TIME

In the early 1990's the Social Work Department embarked upon an extensive re-organisation programme in Edinburgh with some posts disappearing whilst others were created. Amongst the new posts which emerged, four were set up to manage substitute family care services throughout the city, i.e., Adoption, Fostering, Day Care etc. And amazingly, the one established in the Leith sector, where I lived, was only a three quarter time post. I can't really remember why this was but I duly applied and was appointed Resource Team Manager in October '92 with an office situated only ten minutes or so from my home! This new

87

development proved a literal God-send as, in addition to having a quarter of my working week becoming available for TELit, I could also nip home at the occasional lunch time to check proofs, make phone calls - no mobile for me in those days - or despatch orders. With additional time now at my disposal, production continued to increase and by the end of '92 we were on course to see our first million folders into print. But this wasn't the only restructuring to take place at this stage in our development.

RESTRUCTURING... FOR SPACE

It was great to have some extra time to devote to TELit, but I was still left with the problem of space. There was no room in our little house for a study, and yet I badly needed some area or other where I could do all the necessary origination and administration. As the work was increasing so were the number

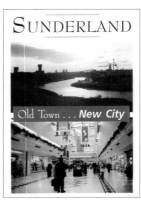

The biggest single project of 1993 - 100,000 copies

of boxes of folders we needed to have available from which to make up orders. This meant that we had boxes all over the house: in the attic, under the beds, in the corners of each room and on every step of our stairs!

But then a fellow Elder at Charlotte Chapel threw us a lifeline. David Whitlie ran a financial services business with an office in Newhaven and offered the use of his basement for storage as well as admin accommodation. This was a wonderful gesture and we were so grateful to

him for such kindness. This gave us much needed breathing space, and proved extremely helpful. However it was difficult to spend too much time there as it was very cold in the winter months and there were a bit too many giant spiders for my liking! But although this certainly solved the storage problem in the short-term, we still needed to find somewhere that could provide suitable desk space. Then one day Maureen had a flash of inspiration.

Our kitchen was 'L' shaped which meant that with some structural re-organisation we could annex part of this by adding a partition and door. This created a form of walk-in cupboard where I could 'escape' in order to do any creative writing, etc.

This proved a great benefit, although I would have to admit that such accessibility made it all too easy for me to work on some TELit project or other during the evenings and weekends. The problem was that our clients had no idea as to the conditions under which I was trying to provide an acceptable service and I felt under pressure to match the response times and general professionalism of other literature producers. It was therefore with a sense of amusement that one day, only two years after the work began, I saw TELit referred to in a Christian magazine as a 'Publishing House'. Little did they know..!

OTHER LOGISTICAL PROBLEMS

Of course, living in a narrow cul-de-sac had other limitations, especially for deliveries. On one occasion I saw a lorry driver phone his office from the foot of our street as he couldn't believe he was being asked to deliver so many boxes to a private house! On another occasion when we were taking delivery of 100,000 folders we had to ask the Lord to prevent it raining over Leith until we got everything safely inside.

There were also problems for our postman, who we came to know very well! He told me that on many occasions he had nothing to deliver to the cul-de-sac, especially when making lunch-time deliveries (remember them?) and yet there seemed to be always something for number 8! (Our postman actually went on to become a Christian, and in a strange turn of events he and his fiance later formed part of a

No 8 in the foreground. Does this look like a publishing house to you?

marriage preparation group that Maureen and I led at Charlotte Chapel).

Now able to spend a quarter of my working week on TELit, I was surprised by how often my concentration was interrupted.

Working from home I was amazed to discover just how many people would call at my door throughout the day. Meter readers, catalogue distributers, double glazing sales people... the list goes on and on. But this extra time was worth its weight in gold.

Now for a while I'd had the spiritual well-being of my elderly neighbour in mind and wondered how I might get a TELit folder into her hands. No natural opportunity seemed to be forthcoming until one day I had a visit from a couple of Jehovah's Witnesses. The net result was that I agreed to accept a piece of their literature, if they were prepared to accept mine. The deal was done and they went on their way. But you can imagine my surprise when a week or so later my neighbour told me that she'd been given a TELit folder by two Jehovah's Witnesses who had called at her door and she'd found it very interesting. The Lord certainly does move in mysterious ways.

Of course, working from home brought other complications. When answering the phone we didn't know whether to announce ourselves as the Sprotts or TELit, having no separate number for the Trust at this stage. As our telephone number was printed on each folder, thus generating many orders, we also found it necessary to have a telephone extension by the bed. This helped us deal with the occasional abusive call, although as the fax machine was downstairs the periodic communication from Australia proved a bit more disruptive in the middle of the night!

MORE GROWTH AND MORE CHANGE

Things developed well under these circumstances and the work continued to expand. And yet a big disappointment was just around the corner.

As the work was growing, I wondered if I might dare to consider the possibility of working full-time with TELit. If I had been single and without three young daughters I would have taken the risk, but as the family breadwinner I was much more hesitant. Faced with the following dilemma, this was a period of great uncertainty. I knew that I could be so much more productive were I to have additional time to devote to TELit. And yet, on the other hand, the wrong move at this stage could spell disaster for the family, so caution won the day. As any father should, I had a strong sense of responsibility, especially for my delightful wee girls and looking back, my heart is full of praise and gratitude to the Lord for the way He has sustained us.

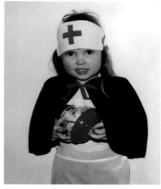
Joanna in 1983

The years have flown by as each of our daughters has become a lovely young lady. They inherited their grandfather's musical ability and in due course each became leader of the Leith Academy school orchestra. After graduating from Glasgow University with a Masters in Chemistry, Joanna is now working as a systems analyst in Manchester. Rachel became a primary school teacher and married John Percival in 2009. He served as a pastor to the London business community from St. Peter's Barge moored at Canary Wharf and in 2010 they moved to Hong Kong, responding to a call to lead an international church. Rebekah is our only daughter still living in Edinburgh. She married Graham Penman, also in 2009, and works for the City of Edinburgh Council's Social Care Service (Children and Families).

And yet, things could have been so different if I had run ahead of the Lord's timing. However, as a basic principle I've always felt that if we obey the Lord in the general, day-to-day issues of life, He will take care of the particulars for us. And this was borne out through the following unexpected incident, through which the Lord *appeared* to be saying to us 'No'.

Rachel in 1985

One day I received a call from a man who had previous experience in financial planning whilst working for a large publishing company in the west of Scotland. He offered to have a look at our accounts with a view to helping us determine the way ahead. Feeling that this seemed a timely development I readily welcomed his offer, cautiously anticipating a positive outcome. However, having thoroughly considered all of our costs and charges etc, he was convinced that our margins

were simply far too small for us to consider any reduction in my hours of secular employment. And yet I knew that we would lose valuable business if we were to increase our prices at this stage. I was hugely disappointed but committed our way to the Lord, got my head down and went on with the work at hand.

Around this time Dorothy Bartlett, one of our Trustees, asked me how long I thought it might take

Rebekah in 1991

for things to reach the stage where I could be employed full-time with TELit. I remember thinking that as things stood, it would be many years, if ever at all. But circumstances were to take another unexpected twist, and instead of having said 'No', perhaps the Lord had been saying 'Not yet'.

The social work staff team I managed began to agitate in favour of my post being increased to full-time. I had to admit that they had a good case for this and yet I knew that it would be a retrograde step for TELit. Of course when it came to the prospect of a Departmental cost increase of this nature nothing happened very quickly and therefore this issue festered on for several months before it was ultimately agreed in principle by senior management. During this time I was playing things cool whilst praying them hot! Despite such uncertainty I felt reluctant to ask Maureen what she felt we should do. On the one hand she knew that I would like to leave the Department altogether, whilst on the other she probably considered it premature or even foolhardy from a financial point of view. It would have put her in a horrible position. So I said nothing to her about this and left it all in the Lord's hands.

Now it so happened that I was booked to take part in a conference down south and had to be away for a few days. Well, by my return, Maureen had been through the busiest three days of TELit admin thus far. And without my having to raise the subject with her, she was now convinced that the time had come to seriously consider stepping out in faith with TELit. This also felt like divine confirmation for me as, without my having tried to influence Maureen in this direction, it looked as though the Lord had graciously taken the matter out of my hands. With the work continuing to expand we mobilised prayer amongst friends and family. In due course all came back urging us to 'go for it'. Which is of course what we did.

So, having worked for Lothian Regional Council for the previous 18 years and 5 months, I left for good and became full-time General Secretary of the TELit Trust in April 1994. This was a dream come true. After all, how many of us are given the wonderful privilege of earning our living from our hobby?

We had worked out that TELit could afford to pay me a modest salary which, coupled with Maureen's childminding fees, would enable us to get by. However, it's one thing living by faith when in receipt of a Local Authority credit transfer each month, yet another when this is suddenly removed! But then, the safest place this side of heaven is always the centre of God's will and we knew in our hearts that so long as we kept in step with the Spirit He wouldn't let us down. And of course we had His precious promise of adequate provision....

> *"...do not worry, saying, 'What shall we eat?' or 'What shall we drink?' or 'What shall we wear?' ...your heavenly Father knows that you need them. But seek first his kingdom and his righteousness, and all these things will be given to you as well."*
> **Matthew 6: 31-33**

By surrendering our finances to Him day by day any sense of anxiety was lifted from us. As time went on we found that without ever asking for financial help funds began to be provided for the work and for us. We received one-off gifts and some regular support, at times from the most unlikely of people. The Lord saw to it that we never received so little as to be unable to respond to outreach opportunities or so much that we ceased to trust Him completely for our livelihood and the well-being of TELit.

Chapter 16

The Acquisition of Premises

'Ask and it will be given to you; seek and you will find; knock and the door will be opened to you.'

Matthew 7:7

In the early 1990's TELit began to really take off. By 1991 we'd produced a total of 265,000 evangelistic folders. Production increased by a further 443,000 in 1992 and by another 580,000 in 1993. I began working full-time for TELit in April '94, exactly 20 years after having become a Christian. And now the level of printing and sales increased even more, as did every other feature of the work.

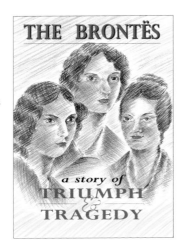

The first folder to have been produced after having begun work for TELit full-time

Working from home was necessary at this stage due to prevailing financial circumstances but this was also bringing its own problems.

In addition to looking after our own young children, Maureen was childminding several others in an effort to augment the family income. This meant that although I would try to hide myself away in my 'cupboard off the kitchen' distractions were inevitable. Space was also becoming an increasing problem, not just for TELit but also for us as a family. Rachel and Rebekah were still sharing a bedroom but each was really needing a room of their own. The bulk of our stock was still held in the basement in Newhaven and therefore access to this was at minimum a half hour round trip away. So Maureen and I began to pray for the Lord's guidance as to the way ahead. And in November 1994, just seven short months after beginning to work full-time for the Trust, the Lord seemed to step in quite decisively.

UNEXPECTED GIFT

Out of the blue we received a gift of £500 from someone who knew something of our situation but wasn't closely connected to the work. This gift came with the stipulation that it be used towards the acquisition of premises and as such formed the basis of a Premises Fund. At this time the Trustees were also firmly of the mind that it would be beneficial if there could be a physical separation made between my work and the domestic scene. This was because distinctions between the two were becoming increasingly blurred, to the detriment of family life.

Although I was afraid that we might be trying to accomplish too much too quickly, it seemed as though we were now on course for another major step forward. In parallel with this Maureen and I also felt that we had to find more adequate accommodation for our family. So there we were, looking for business and domestic premises, pretty much at the same time.

Although we had a fairly good idea as to what we needed as a family, it was much more difficult to assess what would be required for TELit. But I was able to narrow this down a bit in my own mind as I knew that certain features would be essential:

1. We needed our new family home to be near the schools our girls were attending and therefore it would be advantageous for the TELit office to be reasonably nearby.

2. We needed a geographical location that would facilitate deliveries and collections from carriers, as well as an address that would not prove too difficult to find if clients were to visit us in person.

3. We needed somewhere not too large as to be unrealistic nor too small so as to mean a further move all too soon.

4. We needed premises that would offer adequate storage space; an office facility from where I could do all the organisational and administrative work, and if there could be some form of showroom facility, then that would be a bonus.

5. We needed somewhere on ground level, for obvious reasons, and would provide, we reckoned, around 1000 sq. ft of floor space.

It was decided to purchase if at all possible rather than lease as this seemed the better form of stewardship. But of course there was little we could do in a practical sense until sufficient funding became available.

Over the next few months the Premises Fund began to grow but then seemed to get stuck around the £3,000 mark. Now our Chairman at the time, Donald Cameron, was by nature a man of action. Always anxious to do what he could to further any cause in the interests of the gospel, he seized the initiative. With the approval of his fellow Trustees, he took a supply of TELit letterheadings and wrote to a number of those around the Chapel encouraging them to recognise in a tangible way this opportunity to further the work of the gospel. To this day I have never seen the letter he wrote but as the weeks went by we received gift after gift. So much so that by the summer of '95 we felt we had sufficient funds to press ahead with a purchase.

THE PROPERTY SEARCH

With a rough idea as to the kind of place we were looking for, we began to consider a number of properties in the north of the city.

Nearby Leith Links - true home of golf

On one particular evening I was driving around Leith looking at various 'For Sale' signs on a number of buildings. It was getting late and as I drove slowly along a stretch of properties where several were for sale, out of the gathering gloom a shadowy figure appeared from a doorway. To my horror I suddenly realised that I was being approached by a local 'Lady of the night'! She obviously took me to be a kerb crawler and recognised what she thought to be a business opportunity.

Needless to say my interest in the property from whose doorway she had emerged evaporated immediately and I beat a hasty retreat.

We subsequently narrowed the search down to three properties. And yet there seemed to be features of each one that didn't seem quite right for us. Then one day my mother-in-law reminded me of a shop situated towards the Leith end of Ferry Road that had stood empty for quite some time. I had driven past this place on a number of occasions but had always thought of it as being too small. And yet on closer examination I realised that initial appearances can be deceptive - a principle that I was to discover was true, not only of people, but also of premises!

144a FERRY ROAD

This place consisted of a retail/showroom area to the front, leading back up a short staircase to a good-sized room, ideal for an office, and then further back through a corridor to a large square room at the rear, the perfect place to store stock and make up orders. All in all there was a little over 1,000 square feet of floor space, just what we seemed to need. And the sizeable basement was a welcome and unexpected bonus from the Lord.

Facilities were rather primitive when we first moved in!

The market for commercial property of this nature was not particularly buoyant at this time and therefore we concluded what we felt was a very good deal.

By now Maureen and I had also settled on a new family home, though selling 8 Noble Place was quite a struggle. In the light of all the anticipated upheaval I remember one of our Trustees, Jeremy, telling me that he had asked the Lord for us to be allowed access to the new TELit base in Ferry Road first, so that we would avoid having to move all the TELit stuff twice! And this is exactly what happened. A week before we moved as a family, the Venture Scouts from Charlotte Chapel in a convoy of cars took everything that belonged to TELit from Noble Place, and the Newhaven basement, to our new premises.

Our new home in 1995

And exactly one year on from when we received that first gift towards the acquisition of premises, I began work from what were to become the worldwide headquarters of TELit!

FURNITURE, FITTINGS AND EQUIPMENT

When we first moved in we were faced with little more than a shell of a building, and yet it was truly wonderful to have space, real space. Although funds were tight we managed to steadily improve the fabric and appearance of the place through careful housekeeping and the generosity of the Lord's people.

As a condition of the insurance cover we needed to instal an intruder alarm system at the front and back of the building. We were also required to fit roller shutters over our two large windows which face onto Ferry Road. In fact we had some joinery work carried out early on to enable us to mount opened-out TELit folders onto display boards so that members of the public could stop and read these. And by having special sections cut out of the shutters, passers-by could stop and read the content of these folders, even when our premises were closed. Presenting the gospel through the windows in this way has proved a very positive initiative. Hundreds of people have been able to stop and read a presentation of the gospel - especially when the City of Edinburgh Council in their wisdom decided to

locate a temporary bus stop right outside our front door.
As word of our new premises got around the Christian
community of Edinburgh we
began to receive various
offers of much-needed help.

When I began to work from
Ferry Road winter was
beginning to kick-in and with
no heating in the building
I made myself a pair of
fingerless woollen gloves
in the style of those made
famous by Albert Steptoe!
But within a few weeks we
received a telephone call
out of the blue from a

Window display from outside...

Christian organisation in the city offering us four storage heaters
which were now surplus to their requirements. They were
literally a God-send and three are still operational today.

A Christian joiner, Angus Gardner, who lived nearby, carried out
some essential work for us in a most professional way. His was

craftsmanship
of the highest
order and he
refused to make
any charge apart
from the cost of
materials, saying
that it gave him
pleasure to see
his skills used
in support of the
Lord's work.

...and inside!

The interior of our building needed to be painted throughout
and this was carried out by two Christian painters, George
Orphant and his business partner Alastair Moxey. Now George
had been a professional footballer in days gone by playing for
Hearts and East Fife. (I realised that I'd actually seen him play
at Methil when I was about 12!) In the course of the work

he brought along some of his memorabilia, and we sat together on the floor one lunch time and amongst all the cans of paint took a wonderful walk down memory lane together.

Throughout this period, although our financial resources were very limited, we never lacked for anything that we really needed. Whilst it was necessary to purchase the likes of carpeting, much of the more basic practical work I carried out myself. This is unlike a friend of mine who told me that for all his DIY needs he has the three perfect tools - his telephone, pen and cheque book! We were also given various items of office furniture, fittings and stationery.

Our new staircase - built by Angus

All had proved surplus to requirements elsewhere but were most gratefully received by TELit.

One item which proved a bit more difficult to acquire however was racking suitable for storing what was becoming an enormous number of boxes. Glancing through a copy of Industrial Exchange and Mart one day I spotted what looked just the thing for us - heavy duty

A section of our multi-coloured heavy-duty racking

steel racking from a Government establishment which had closed down. So a week or two later it arrived on a lorry from Nottingham - a huge pile of filthy scrap iron! But in the course of an evening, along with a bunch of friends, it was cleaned up and we went on to have great fun assembling it like some great overgrown Meccano set!

And after I had painted it one Saturday morning - each section a different colour - it looked great!

THE BASEMENT - POSSIBLE OPTIONS

At the beginning we didn't really need the space offered by the basement, which was probably just as well because every time there was rain, it leaked like a sieve. However we reckoned that it was a resource that the Lord had given us and as such it should be put to use. So we had it made watertight and considered various options.

One proposal was to turn it into an internet cafe for young people and a very dear friend, Harry Robertson, who is a draughtsman by profession, drew up some plans. However this was to be a non-starter due to difficulties with public access.

Instead we've used it over the years as a storage facility for members of Charlotte Chapel who, for one reason or another, have found themselves 'in transit' and needed somewhere to store belongings for a while. In fact, this has become so well used that it's not uncommon to see five or six sets of belongings stored there at any one time!

We had also considered trying to make wider use of the retail section to the front of our building. We wondered if we should sell crafts and cards etc, in an attempt to attract more of the Christian public of Edinburgh. However, we decided against this for various reasons and over time this has proved to have been the right decision. As the work has developed we've needed all the space available for purely TELit activities.

OPEN DAY

Once most of the renovation and equipping was completed

OPEN
DAY
----------<>----------
INVITATION
----------<>----------
Saturday 15th
November 1997

we felt we'd like to have the premises consecrated in a formal way. This took place in the course of a special Open Day held on Saturday 15 November 1997.

The senior pastor of Charlotte Chapel, Rev Peter Grainger, conducted a short dedication ceremony and thereafter

Open Day visitors

many friends and supporters had a good time looking around the place and enjoying fellowship together.

To see so many whose spiritual calibre I greatly admired be

More Open Day visitors

prepared to give up their Saturday afternoon in this way was truly humbling, and I felt so unworthy. But then, TELit has never been about me.

It was amazing to realise just how much the work had moved on in such a short time.

THE LORD PROVIDES - YET AGAIN!

Over the years we've always considered these premises to have been the Lord's and not ours. And from day one the building has always seemed just right in terms of space and location. We've been very grateful for all the help we've received in equipping and maintaining the property and thankfully we've always managed to meet our running costs. Even in 2007 when we were faced with a massive roof repair bill we managed to cope somehow with this exceptional expense.

Before

After

Over the years we've suffered very little in terms of vandalism. There have been those who have spat on our front windows of course and others have thrown eggs, but apart from a spate of broken windows to the rear we've survived remarkably unscathed... and this despite our being an overtly Christian establishment situated on a major thoroughfare.

Perhaps the key to this has been the faithfulness of those who pray for us, and especially Marion, a dear elderly lady who promised to pray for the building from the very day on which she heard that the Lord had entrusted it to us. But as she has now gone to be with Him, perhaps we should brace ourselves for a bit more trouble, unless of course the Lord raises up someone else to fulfil this important role.

Chapter 17

Family Matters

'It is not good for the man to be alone. I will make a helper suitable for him.'

Genesis 2:18

When the full story of TELit is eventually revealed in Eternity it will become clear just how vital has been the contribution made by one person in particular - my wife Maureen.

Maureen at Lochgoilhead 2008

Her role in the 'success' of the work has been unspectacular yet crucial, and no doubt in the final analysis she will be considered an unsung heroine in the growth, development and progress of TELit. Her sensitive spiritual discernment and solid practical judgement have proved tremendous assets in both major and minor decision-making. I can't think of anyone else who would have stood with me so faithfully and effectively through all the ups and downs, especially as she has complemented so well my superabundance of shortcomings!

MY GREATEST NEED

Over the years many people have referred to what they have perceived to be a special gift I've received from the Lord to communicate the gospel through literature. They may well be right, and that's because as a general principle the Lord never calls any of us to serve Him in some special way without also providing the necessary ability. However, the idea that 'publishable' prose simply flows from my pen every day is wide of the mark to say the least! You see, vital to the whole operation is not money, people, premises or even my physical health. No, the greatest need that TELit has, and has always had, is that I maintain a right relationship with the Lord. In fact, those who pray for me in this way are doing TELit the greatest good. I have no doubt about this whatsoever, because, as I look back over my life, I would echo the words of evangelist D.L. Moody who said:

> *'I have never met a man who has given me as much trouble as myself.'*

And of course this is where Maureen makes such an important contribution to the work. It's been said that we all get to know ourselves better through one another. And having had her by my side has not only been a wonderful experience for me in so many ways but a vitally important factor in the development of TELit. Yet from the very beginning we seemed a most unlikely and even an oddly-matched couple. And for this to be fully appreciated I need to explain something about the emotional and psychological complexities of my earlier life.

HEALING AND WHOLENESS

Like all of us I'm a product of nature and nurture. And as I said at the very beginning of this book, had I been God, I wouldn't have chosen me for TELit, far from it. I would have considered Barry Sprott highly unsuitable for Christian service of any kind. And even now I wonder why someone far more appropriate wasn't chosen for work of such magnitude. I say this because in addition to my complete lack of formal training in the likes of graphic art, theology or English language, when I became a Christian I brought with me an

I tried to put a brave face on things during much of the late 60's / early 70's

enormous amount of baggage, mostly of an emotional nature.

Dumbarton's Glasgow Road - where the now long gone Cafe Continental was for my friends and me the local meeting place back in the mid 60's

Whilst living in Dumbarton I had a brief relationship with a girl who I considered to be the most beautiful in the world. But all too soon this faltered - for which I blamed myself - and on returning to Kirkcaldy absence made my heart grow even fonder. Our broken romance began to become an unhealthy pre-occupation for me. In fact I would go so far as to say that it became an obsession. I felt chained to her memory, even though I knew that her affections had moved on, and that she had met and married someone else.

With Morag from Kirkcaldy - to whom I might have become engaged in the early 70's

Throughout the following eight years or so I had many more relationships varying in duration and intensity with some truly lovely girls. Yet I was unable to sustain any of these because memories of this particular girl proved an insurmountable obstacle. My thoughts were determining my feelings and therefore her rejection haunted me, though I couldn't understand why. It was as if I was echoing the words of Pascal when he asserted:

106

'The heart has its reasons of which reason knows nothing.'

As time went by I just couldn't break free from a persistent sense of loss and regret. They say that the key to good mental health is for us to be pretty much the same on the 'outside' of our lives as we are on the 'inside'. But I'd have to admit that this was yet another difficult area for me. Weighed down by a daily burden of sadness I did my best to conceal my inner reality from friends and family, though I was only moderately successful.

I've gone on to realise of course that it was in the gracious providence of God that my family left Dumbarton in 1965. In this way I was spared surely one of the most harrowing experiences that any of us might ever be asked to endure - to watch the person we love, love someone else. I could readily identify with Brent Curtis who describes in *The Sacred Romance* a very similar experience in his life...

> **'However the Haunting comes, it often brings with it a bitter sweet poignancy of ache, the sense that we stood at a crossroads somewhere in the past and chose a turning that left some shining part of ourselves - perhaps the best part - behind...'**

And then, after referring in more detail to his own lost love...

> **'And each of us has points of contact where the transcendence of the Romance has seared our heart in the fragrance of lovers, geographies and times. They are captured there and return to haunt us with their loss whenever we return, or are returned, to their heart locale.'**

So on 26th April 1974 when I cried out to the Lord I had reached the point of desperation, and, on reflection, felt as the Psalmist must have done when he wrote:

> **'How long must I wrestle with my thoughts and every day have sorrow in my heart?'**
> **Psalm 13:2**

My experience was similar in some ways to that of C.S. Lewis (of Narnia fame) who in his 1955 autobiography *Surprised by Joy* described himself at the point of his conversion as *'the most dejected and reluctant convert in all of England'*. I too was a disconsolate, despairing, pathetic soul, and the words of Bill and Gloria Gaither's song *Something Beautiful* summed me up perfectly:

> **'If ever there were dreams that were lofty and noble, they were my dreams at the start; And the hopes for life's best were the hopes that I harboured down deep in my heart. But my dreams turned to ashes, my castles all crumbled, my fortune turned to loss. So I wrapped it all in the rags of my life, and laid it at the Cross!'**

In becoming a Christian I surrendered everything to the Lord, including all my affections, desires and aspirations. The Holy Spirit coming to live in my life made me feel brand new, clean and free from the shackles that had held me. To my surprise I received a special quality of peace, acceptance and reassurance. And although these wonderful blessings didn't include complete healing of my anguished psyche there and then, I knew I had placed my life into loving hands that would one day see my restoration complete.

EMOTIONAL RENAISSANCE

Over the years my emotional attachments have been put into

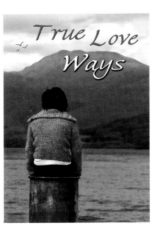

proper perspective as the Lord has rehabilitated my private world. With this in mind, back in 2004 I borrowed the title of the beautiful Buddy Holly song *True Love Ways* and produced a folder specifically for the benefit of those who feel that their hearts have been broken beyond repair. From the day on which I became a true Christian the Lord began the process of helping me reorder my emotional life. And I knew that what He could do for me He could do for others. However I still believe that it's better to accept the vulnerability of loving someone and risk a broken heart because, in the words of J.M. Barrie: '...*even love unreturned has its rainbow'*.

In placing my life under the authority and management of the Lord, I was also going on to prove a principle made explicit by Hudson Taylor, founder of the China Inland Mission (now OMF). It's a principle which can be applied to every aspect of life, and has certainly been true of my relationship with Maureen:

'God always gives His very best to those who leave the choice with Him.'

Opposites do attract and over the years Maureen and I have tended to fill the voids in each other's lives. I've always felt that she and I were right for each other, long before TELit was even an idea in my head. But it also shows how God can be preparing us for special tasks and projects before we ever realise it.

Maureen and I are very different in many ways, one of which is temperament. She always seems to see the glass half full, whilst I'm more likely see it half

Maureen, preparing to do some work on the dreaded computer!

empty! Though I wouldn't consider myself unduly depressive, all too easily I can lose my spiritual buoyancy, to the detriment of TELit. And time and time again the Lord has encouraged and reassured me through Maureen. But we also differ in other ways. She received a far more 'Christian' up-bringing than I did, in terms of personal faith. As a consequence she had, and still has, a better knowledge of the Scriptures. In this way, she's been well able to check my theology over the years and make very astute and welcome - well, sometimes welcome - suggested adjustments to what I've written.

109

Maureen, and indeed all three daughters, have never been slow to express a constructive opinion regarding any prototype publication I've decided to run by them. This has been so helpful whether in terms of a title, choice of illustrations or even a particular turn of phrase. There's no doubt that over the years we've borne out the wisdom of Solomon:

> *'Plans fail for lack of counsel, but with many advisers they succeed'.*
> **Proverbs 15:22**

Maureen is also very much a 'people person' with a natural antipathy towards computers. But just as she's developed an appreciation of football over the years we've been together, so she's been willing to take on a number of admin tasks around the office on a voluntary basis.

Yet our many natural differences are insignificant compared to all that unites us as Christians. Over the 36 years we've known each other, the Lord has moulded us together as only He could, so much so that our differences are not irksome but positively refreshing. All in all I reckon we've developed a very fruitful partnership in the Lord's grace, and it's been such a privilege to go through this great adventure together.

MY DAUGHTERS

Joanna

Our three girls were all brought up with TELit an integral feature of family life. And as they grew older the Trust benefited from their enthusiasm to boost their personal finances through doing some of the most boring, mundane, mind-numbing tasks associated with the work.

Over the years all three have been 'employed' on a sessional basis. Each has spent long hours helping with stocktaking, mailshots, overprinting, collating statistics... sticking, stuffing and folding... and probably wishing that the government hadn't taken so long to establish the National Minimum Wage! Each of our daughters is such a blessing to us and has made their own valuable contribution to the productivity of TELit.

On the down side however I'm all too aware that being brought

Rachel

up in a household where the full-time employment of the main breadwinner is of an overtly Christian character brings its own unique challenges. It can be very costly from a number of perspectives. This is because we have a spiritual enemy who is strong and active, manifesting his attacks in very subtle yet destructive ways. He wants to destroy the work of TELit, and where he might consider Maureen and I to be a bit more likely to withstand some of his personal assaults, he will all too often see our girls as softer, easier targets. As Christian parents we're therefore so grateful to those who pray for our daughters on a regular basis, and indeed for us all as a family.

IMPACT ON FAMILY LIFE

From the very outset of TELit I've had a heightened sense of how important family life should be to those of us in this type of work. What a sad indictment it is when precious relationships with those closest to us are steadily eroded through the legitimate demands of a developing Christian ministry.

Rebekah

Looking back I've always tried to take a hands-on attitude to family life in general and the upbringing of our children in particular. I was there when each was born, did my fair share of nappy-changing, helped to put them to bed most nights and made sure I never missed a school parents' evening. As their father I've never wanted to give them cause to question my love and devotion so that they could be sure I would always be there for them, no matter what. And of course the greatest kindness I could offer in order to help develop their sense of security has been to love and cherish their mother.

Maureen and I always wanted our family home to be warm, welcoming and full of fun. In fact, I used to encourage foster carers to develop a strong sense of humour as this would see them through many a sticky domestic situation.

We also liked to take opportunities to provide hospitality and in due course we've developed a wide circle of treasured friends. The knock-on of this has been to the benefit of our own children who in turn have gone on to establish fulfilling lives. Like most parents we wanted our daughters to reach their full potential both academically and in other ways. And yet we've valued, as more important than all this world has to offer, their personal faith and Christian character. After all, beauty of character - the hidden person of the heart - remains long after the anti-aging cream begins its losing battle with time.

Thankfully, in the providence of God, I've never been drawn to a time-consuming activity or interest that took me away from home for long periods. And although sacrifices have had to be made over the years, we feel that the Lord has honoured our attempts to prioritise to His glory.

Children are a gift from God, though Maureen and I have never seen them as a possession, rather as a trust. And although we've failed in many ways to be the parents we've aspired to be, love has always brought harmony even in times of discord.

FRUITFULNESS

The Lord's blessing

Chapter 18

Publicising the Product

*'Cast your bread upon the waters, for after many days
you will find it again.'*

Ecclesiastes 11:1

By the mid 1990's the work was really flourishing. I was the full-time General Secretary of the Trust; we had our own premises on Ferry Road, and orders were arriving thick and fast, broadly within two categories.

Firstly, there would be special commissions. These took the form of an approach from a particular individual, church or organisation requesting something totally unique and committing themselves to the entire print run. In these circumstances we would normally charge a design fee, given that specific projects always involve a great deal of origination work on my part. Such requests have resulted in titles like 'Keep On Running', for the London to Brighton Veteran Car Run; 'Harbour Lights', for the Tall Ships Race 2005 on the River Tyne and, 'Have you got.. THE KNOWLEDGE?', for London City Mission's work amongst taxi drivers.

 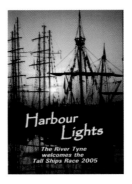 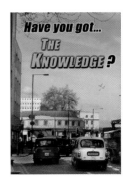

Examples of special commissions.

Many publications have been developed in this way over the years yet most will never have been seen by our supporters or client base. Nevertheless, folders of this nature have always formed an important aspect of TELit's ministry and their uniqueness has helped fulfil our objective to demonstrate the relevance of the gospel within a very specific context.

The other major category would be formed by those titles which have been initiated by ourselves. Taking such general themes as the environment, family life or the financial services, evangelistic folders have been produced which have gone on to be updated and reprinted on many occasions. One such an example is 'Reason to Believe', our publication designed specifically for young people.

Our folder for young people has been produced in a number of versions over the years

I consider this to be one of our most important designs as the teenage years are such a critical stage in life. This is the point where attitudes are formed and values established which can go on to determine an entire lifestyle pattern. And therefore how important it is to relate the gospel to issues relevant within this context. After all, so many young people today have little or no accurate understanding or appreciation of the gospel and without realising it may go on to throw away their lives. They'll do this, not necessarily through the misuse of drugs or alcohol or even suicide. Many will choose a truly altruistic aim, perhaps a career in healthcare or develop a passion for education, but then, at the end of the day, and when it's too late to do anything about it, they'll realise they've chosen the wrong aim. Through 'Reason to Believe' I want young people to realise that God has a plan for each of our lives but we won't discover this by leaving Him out of it. The good can so easily become the enemy of the best.

Although ideas for such titles are usually the result of simply recognising a contemporary theme which could be developed, I'm always open to the suggestions of others. However, by no means have I acted upon every idea which I've been asked to consider. I'm sufficiently long in the tooth to realise that without the prospect of fairly widespread general appeal, publications will sit on our shelves and gather dust.

THE DEVELOPMENT OF OUR CATALOGUE

It's always been a major challenge to try to engage with the Christian public effectively yet efficiently. We realised from the outset of the work that we needed to market our publications in such a way as to maximise their sales potential. But I knew that the majority of our supporters wanted their particular support to be channelled into producing the finished product rather than to be used for some form of publicity or administration, no matter how essential this might be.

In view of all this, and with our database of those ordering our material beginning to grow, we felt as though TELit was becoming a form of mail order organisation. We therefore decided to send out a regular mailshot four times a year.

Christmas, Easter and Harvest, in that order, have always been

116

major times of year for us in terms of sales. Taking account of this we began to schedule a mailshot for the end of January (for Easter); end of April (summer activities); end of August (Harvest and Christmas overprinting) and early December (Christmas stragglers!). But we needed to decide what to send out.

In the very early days we issued a single A4 sheet printed in black only which formed a News/ Prayer letter and also incorporated our range of general titles.

But as the work expanded we could no longer contain every item on this size of sheet. As a result we graduated to a A3

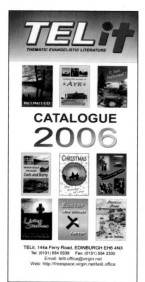

format folded to fit a DL sized envelope, still in black only, and which we now referred to as our Catalogue. Over the years we've experimented with various shapes and sizes but in more recent times we've settled on a full colour A2 layout still folded to fit a DL envelope. This we find to be both adequate and economical, and generates a good return when distributed along with samples of new titles.

SEASONAL PUBLICATIONS

It wasn't long before our clients began to expect us to produce a new Christmas and Easter title each year. These are designed to present a clear and concise overview of all the essential elements of the gospel but we also consider them to be unique in one particular way.

Although I initiated the work of TELit (perhaps it would be more accurate to say that the Lord initiated it through me) I certainly haven't been responsible for all the good ideas that we've implemented over the years. And one in particular relates to our Christmas and Easter folders. It was one of our earlier chairmen, Donald Cameron, who first suggested devoting a page

The Christmas title 'Reason for the Season' remains a favourite and has had numerous reprints

of these publications to the possible overprinting of a church's Christmas or Easter activities, thus creating an invitation to their special services. In this way, though the recipient may not accept the invitation per se, they would still receive a presentation of the gospel. To my mind this seems a much more sensible and potentially productive use of time and money than simply circulating some form of flyer round the neighbourhood which only gives the most basic of practical information.

This approach has proved enormously successful, judging by the hundreds of thousands, perhaps millions, which have been produced in this way. And we've received very positive feedback as a result of their use.

PROMOTING THE POTENTIAL

I've always been convinced that our product is our most powerful advert, so it's been our aim to do what we can to get at least one evangelistic folder into the hands of Christians who as yet know nothing of TELit whatsoever.

Accompanied by a sample title, the 'Introducing TELit' brochure not only features our range of products, but also explains something of the ethos underpinning the work. And from time to time we've put together a mailshot targeting many of the biggest churches in the UK.

However, I would have to admit to having been pretty disappointed with the level of response to much of this promotional activity. Though we receive a regular stream of enquiries, many never materialise beyond this stage. And even

the use of our 'Freepost Enquiry Response Card' rarely gives us any insight into why prospective users decide against ordering. Christians are notoriously bad at giving an honest explanation in such circumstances and would rather say nothing at all, probably for fear of appearing negative. And yet this attitude doesn't really help us. We need to know how to scratch where people itch.

I guess that in all of this, I struggle to understand why so many Christians seem so reluctant to convey the essentials of the gospel through TELit material to our confused and perplexed

society. Perhaps too many of us have lost sight of all we're told in the Bible that lies ahead for those who are bound for a lost Eternity. Yet were we to be given a glimpse into hell I'm sure that our flagging zeal would see such a transformation.

Chapter 19

Material for Children

'Love the LORD your God with all your heart and with all your soul and with all your strength. These commandments that I give you today are to be upon your hearts. Impress them on your children.'

Deuteronomy 6:5-7

The design and production of good outreach literature for children is a spiritual art and I have never considered myself adequately gifted in this direction. For that reason only material for adults was produced throughout our first seven years. However, in 1997 things were to change in this respect, largely in the light of the following:

    1. PUBLIC DEMAND - We were beginning to receive quite consistently, enquiries and requests from existing clients and others for literature which would help children of primary school age understand the basics of the gospel.

    2. INADEQUATE RESOURCES - We were being told fairly regularly by those running children's missions, camps and various Sunday School events that there didn't seem to be much already available to reinforce, in a more permanent way, the gospel message which was being communicated in spoken form.

    3. DIVINE INSPIRATION - It's been said that the Lord sometimes doesn't give us the ticket until we're ready to make the journey. Therefore, it was only after I'd decided to explore this whole scene more seriously that ideas began to germinate.

Leaning heavily upon Maureen's insights, and reflecting upon our experiences with our own children, we decided to 'invent' a couple of wee kids, brother and sister, Josh and Jade. Their parents were orthodox church-going, committed Christians. But their children were typical, ordinary primary school kids whose attitudes and priorities weren't really in keeping with those of their parents.

Our target audience was the age range five to nine broadly speaking, and we felt it to be terribly important that the average school aged child would be able to identify with Josh and Jade in their many escapades.

A REAL LITERARY CHALLENGE

Writing for children is of course very different from writing for adults. Although the basic elements of the gospel to be imparted are the same, a different style of presentation altogether is necessary.

Our first children's title 'Josh and Jade ..in big trouble' in the original 4 part set format

Long words and complex terminology are no good and therefore I was immediately faced with having to produce a product in a different style to that of our adult publications. It also seemed essential to build in an interactive, entertainment factor in the hope of retaining interest.

The net result of all this was our first children's title, 'Josh and Jade ..in big trouble'. This took the form of a four part set with a story running through and a cliffhanger at the end of each part. We also included a number of puzzles to be unravelled and codes to be cracked, as well as offering plenty of colouring-in opportunities.

The artwork for this was produced by two lovely girls - initially Rachel Swanson, and later Sonya Lisowski. These publications began to attract considerable interest and before long it became necessary to develop further adventures for Josh and Jade. The next two sets were 'Josh and Jade ..beat the bully' and 'Josh and Jade ..and the accident'.

EXPANSION AND DEVELOPMENT

These Josh and Jade four part sets proved very popular as they were particularly useful at children's events spread over several days. Nevertheless it wasn't long before we were being asked for a single item version which could be used when one-off opportunities with children were encountered.

This led to the scaling down of the content to form an activity sheet. These still retained all the core content but within a single sheet of A3 size which opened up, rather like road map.

Despite their initial popularity the four part sets have been discontinued within recent years due largely to rising costs and falling sales. However the activity sheets remain popular to the present day and a series of eight titles has been produced thus far. Over the years we've been asked what Josh and Jade

have been up to at Christmas, Easter and Hallowe'en, hence the design and production of specific titles. The most recently produced title is 'Josh and Jade ..get a shock' based on the theme of football.

UNEXPECTED PUBLICITY

We produced our first version of 'Josh and Jade at Hallowe'en' in 1998 and this generated a great deal of media attention. It had been designed to explain the basics of the gospel within the

'Josh and Jade at Hallowe'en'   Sides 1 & 2

context of Hallowe'en whilst at the same time alerting youngsters to something of the darker side of this pagan event.

Our publication had been mentioned in Charlotte Chapel's magazine and this was duly picked up on by the *Edinburgh Evening News* who, after interviewing me, ran an article on it. They, in turn, passed this on to *The Scotsman*, and from there I received requests for interviews from a variety of national newspapers including *The Guardian, The Independent, The Daily Record, The Sun, The Express* etc, etc. I even took part in a live debate on Radio Scotland from my office by telephone.

It seemed that the issue they all wanted to question was my reference to the spiritual dangers inherent within Hallowe'en. (Actually, if you still reckon it's only harmless fun, just type 'Hallowe'en' into any search engine and you'll be left in no doubt as to its true nature... far removed from simply dookin' for apples!)

Most of the media coverage of this ranged from sarcasm to scorn, some of which was really quite hurtful.

I was particularly concerned by the 'do-gooding' references in several articles, though this put me in mind of Scottish theologian William Barclay. I remember his reference to the Japanese poet Kagawa who wrote...

> *'I read in a book about a man called Christ who went about doing good. It is very disconcerting to me that I'm so easily satisfied with just going about.'*

Our intention in producing this activity sheet was to provide Christians with something of true and lasting value which they could give to youngsters along with their bar of chocolate etc, when they come to the door guising. Mind you, maybe it's a sign of the times, but most who come to our door nowadays are really only looking for money!

124

Chapter 20

International Dimension

'All authority in heaven and on earth has been given to me. Therefore go and make disciples of all nations, baptising them in the name of the Father and of the Son and of the Holy Spirit, and teaching them to obey everything I have commanded you.'

Matthew 28:18-20

From the very beginning I knew that the type of outreach literature we were developing had worldwide potential. But in the early days it was more than enough to try to cope with the UK scene alone.

Yet as time went by, and without our having embarked upon any form of international promotional activity, enquiries and even some orders began to trickle in from faraway places. To begin with requests were received for folders only in English from English speaking countries. For example, the Christian

Motorcyclists Association in Australia took a liking for 'Where the Rubber hits the Road'; the Canadian Bible Society used 'Run to Win' and a church in Cape Town commissioned a special printing of 'Family Matters'.

A number of orders have also been received from the USA over the years including a special design for Rochester (home of the Mayo Clinic) in Minnesota.

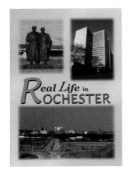

I'm not sure how these folks heard about us, but another early commission resulted from a 'chance meeting' at Charlotte Chapel with the Chaplain to Tourists in Darwin, Australia. He had spotted one of our 'Welcome to Edinburgh' folders in a literature rack and asked if we could produce a similar publication for him to use with his outreach work in Darwin. More recently we've received further commissions for particular centres of population in Australia, largely the result of considerable help from a good friend to TELit based in Lanarkshire.

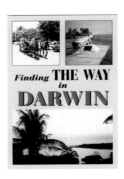

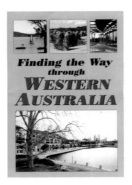

Transportation has always been a major problem in managing to get off-the-shelf publications into the hands of those outside the UK. In some cases carriage costs prove greater than the value of the goods in question and this has no doubt been a disincentive for some wishing to use our material.

On a number of occasions we've tried to establish a partnership arrangement with other Christian publishers in the likes of the USA, Australia or South Africa, but despite our best efforts none has materialised. This has been a disappointment as I'm sure that were our products to become more accessible in these countries they would prove very useful.

However, I can only conclude that this has not been part of the Lord's overall plan and now, on reflection, it would seem that our real value has been in relation to outreach work in some of the far less evangelised regions of the world.

EASTERN EUROPE

As the fall of communism swept across much of Eastern Europe, this opened the way for TELit literature to be used in a number of hitherto hard-to-reach parts of the world. And it has been a great thrill to see our folders translated, produced and circulated in the likes of Russia, Ukraine, Poland, Belarus, Hungary, Romania, Bulgaria and even as far as Siberia, as well as into the Balkan areas of Macedonia and Albania.

Much of this activity originated as a result of word of mouth, with the Lord using certain key individuals to make things happen in respect of particular countries. One good example of a timely encounter was with Stoyan Stoyanov, and this particular divine appointment has led to significant work over many years in Bulgaria.

I met Stoyan for the first time en route to a conference in England.
We had both arrived by train but as he looked rather lost, I asked if I could help him. Discovering that we were both bound for the same destination (in more ways than
one) we shared a taxi. Over the next few days we got to know one another quite well and he began to take a real interest in the

type of literature being produced by TELit.

Since then Stoyan has set up a distribution network throughout
Bulgaria. In 2003 he
emailed me to say:

Bulgarian gypsies reading TELit folders
- international outreach from
Ferry Road in Edinburgh

*'...we wont to tell
you a big Thank
you for the big
help, love and
sacrifice that
you do for all
Bulgarian people.
I didn't find the
word who will
be a right for
your big help for
us. We see how
our Lord work
because we have
more people who
wont to have this folders and also more church who wont
to distribute.*

*We start to distribute in the beginning of this year more
serious distortion for gypsy church also. 15 gypsy's
churches have interest to distribute folders in his nation.
(We make some pictures in gypsy church in villages
Zlokuchene - that mean village Evil Dog in English)*

*Till now we continue to work with 27 regional Pentecostal
churches. They distribute for his satellites churches who
is more than 300. We work also with 19 free charismatic
and 31 single distributors.*

*After finishing quantity people asking when we have
more from this wonderful folders.'*

A pattern has developed whereby each year we print a total of
40,000 folders in Bulgarian, 5,000 each of 8 designs. Production
is financed through our International Outreach Fund and it's
a real privilege to help our Bulgarian brothers and sisters in
this way. This is especially in view of the country's very poor
economic climate as described in another email from Stoyan:

128

'...we must continue to pray because many people in Bulgaria still live very poor. World economic crisis damage a lot of our fragility economic and many people loose his job. We believe that this God's words in the brochures who we give to the people is a really piece of hope for them. This is like gift from the heaven for them. Some of them start to crying and it is so touched.'

Judging by the feedback we've received from various Eastern European countries, evangelism seems to be undertaken much more seriously these days than here in the UK. Perhaps their new found freedom of opportunity has given extra impetus to evangelistic activity and the message of the gospel is considered to be wonderfully precious. For example, I'm told that in Ukraine TELit folders are often pinned up on the walls of the houses!

SPAIN AND PORTUGAL

Whilst the circulation of our publications throughout Eastern Europe has been a wonderful development it's also been a great encouragement to see large quantities of TELit folders used in other parts of the world where the Evangelical Church is comparatively small. For example, we've now seen well over a million folders used in Spain through

172,000 of these were produced for outreach in Portugal during 2004

Spain's bestselling TELit title

our partner organisation, Editorial Peregrino, and a similar arrangement in Portugal through the Christian publisher, Nucleo. In both cases, Christmas and Easter publications have also proved particularly popular, though in Spain 'Bad News for Good People' is TELit's number one best seller.

HIGH PROFILE EVENTS

On some occasions a high profile event will be the springboard for new work beginning in a particular country. An example of this was the Athens Olympics in 2004, which helped provide the initial impetus for what has developed into an important part of our overseas work. In fact, we're told that there are no other publications in Greece similar to TELit folders.

A German Christian using TELit folders to reach English football fans with the gospel!

In the work of the gospel we've learned to expect the unexpected and two very unusual requests from overseas fall into this category.

During the course of an overseas tour some years ago the England Cricket Team were due to have a formal reception in New Delhi. You can imagine my surprise to receive an urgent request from Indian Christians for a quantity of 'Lord of Lord's' in English (though the Hindi version had also been used in India) so that these could be given to the players and their entourage!

Another similar incident arose in the course of the Football World Cup in Germany in 2006. We received a request for 10,000 copies of 'The Winning Goal' in English from German Christians who wished to evangelise the England supporters who would flood into Nuremberg and Stuttgart to see their team in action.

Although sport is a wonderful international 'vehicle' for evangelism, sadly, so is conflict. In recent years we've received several orders for Christmas publications in particular to be included in parcels being sent out to British service personnel in Afghanistan and Iraq.

ASIA

The continent of Asia is a tremendous mission field though a number of the political regimes in positions of power are clearly unsympathetic at best to the work of the gospel. However the ways of man are no match for the King of Kings and Lord of Lords. It's therefore been no real surprise to have seen our publications produced in a number of Asian languages, including Hindi and Urdu. These have gone on to be used, albeit surreptitiously at times, to reach many people with the gospel.

I'd rather not go into too much detail as to where and how our folders are used in this part of the world, but the following excerpt from an email will give something of the flavour of the difficult circumstances under which local Christians engage in evangelism:

Regions prone to hurricanes...

'We need your literatures in our country. Please help us and send the tracts or any booklets and any literature you have. This will help our ministry to reach other people. The literature goes beyond where we can afford. We the minister in ... could not go every where and preach because the sometimes halt and the circumstance made us not to preach. But you literature can preach in the bus, air, house, prison, market, school, office and even in the bedroom.'

...and to earthquakes

It's such a privilege to share the message of God's love, compassion and reconciliation and it's so humbling to receive responses such as the following:

131

'You will be very glad to know that we have translated, published and distributed your book entitled: 'Sow a thought & Reap Destiny' and 'More than Make Over'. Most of them were distributed in Irrawaddy Region where the deadly storm Nargis destroyed. It was over heard that many of them was greatly encouraged by reading this profound articles in the times of shaking down the areas.

There can surely be no greater joy than for a Christian to hear of those bound for a lost Eternity who have found saving faith in the Lord Jesus Christ:

'The folders which have been printed such as Easter, Bad news for good people and Silent Night were so good and were delighted that those were not sufficient. The reader got spiritual discernment and asked for regular delivery. The missionaries testified that our folders were so helpful in their mission works and said that our folders will be the applied material for winning lost souls. The pictures and the high quality can also attract people according to the response. Regards to N.* language folders, we N. people do not have any books nor materials printed in our mother tongue though we have been in 95 years of our Christian age. Since these are the first printed material in N. they say their inner thanks with happy tears. The are some nominal Christians who got born-again through reading our folders Easter, Bad News for good People and Silent Night.'

AFRICA

Over the years we've also received a number of orders from African countries, namely Nigeria, Ghana and Zambia. However, despite subsidy through our International Outreach Fund, transportation costs have proved prohibitive.

The largest single project for an African country thus far has been a special design for the people of Guinea-Bissau. This

WEC missionary and TELit enthusiast - Isa Arthur

*Name of people group omitted.

was at the instigation of some WEC missionaries who sent me photographs of village life and from which we put together a

presentation of the gospel. This was duly translated into the local language, Creole, but due to the underdevelopment of the country as a whole we couldn't find a printer capable of producing what we were looking for.

In view of this we planned to have an initial quantity produced in the UK and then pray for some way to get them over there. We did this, and as it happened, we heard of a missionary family in Northern Ireland who were planning to send a container out to a school in Senegal. When we discovered that the school in question was readily accessible from Guinea-Bissau and that there was space to accommodate our consignment, we praised the Lord for the way that this wonderful opportunity had materialised. Since then two further consignments have been sent amounting to 38,000 folders which we hear have been very well received.

WESTERN EUROPE

The Christian Church has seen significant growth in many parts of the world in recent times, including the Islamic strongholds of the Middle East and North Africa. Yet it's been very sad to see a decline in Western Europe. This trend is also mirrored by TELit as we receive only the occasional order from the likes of Norway, France, Belgium, the Netherlands, etc. But we've been very encouraged to see a steady stream come from the Republic of

Ireland. In addition to requests for off-the-shelf titles we've also been very pleased to produce a number of special designs for specific places.

But Western Europe in general is an area of the world in which TELit struggles to make any real inroads - and not for the want of trying! The potential for literature evangelism would seem enormous with so many capital cities and major centres of population just crying out (to my mind at least) to have a custom-designed evangelistic folder produced for residents and visitors alike. Despite having designed prototypes for the likes of Rome, Ghent, Lisbon and the Algarve, none has so far generated sufficient interest as to justify production. Even the large mission organisations working in these countries express indifference to the prospect of such a unique form of gospel publication. Meanwhile millions of people each year go to a lost Eternity without ever receiving an understanding of the truth.

With an eye to the future, it seems clear to me that the Euro zone

134

is becoming a huge, post-Christian, secular state. And whilst evangelistic activity can be undertaken without too many restrictions at present, time may be running out for such freedom. For example, given the growing popular belief that most of the conflict in the world has its roots in 'religion', one could foresee the day when some European

Bulgarian young people reading TELit material in their own language.

Constitution or Court outlaws the kind of mission work which is possible at present. Therefore, perhaps all the more reason why we need to make the most of current opportunities before it's too late.

INTERNATIONAL POSTSCRIPT

From the outset I had no pre-conceived ideas as to how far the work of TELit would extend. And I still admit to a real sense of amazement to realise that publications written and designed in our modest, unpretentious premises at 144a (not even 144) Ferry Road, Edinburgh, have found their way all over the world. To think that you can be handed a TELit folder on a bus in downtown Yangon (Rangoon) in a language into which the Bible has yet to be translated; that TELit folders have spent a week on a train bound for the frozen outposts of Siberia; that they've been found pinned to the walls of American state penitentiaries; that they're in the hands of holiday makers in the sun-drenched resorts of Kos, Gran Canaria and the Algarve; that through them Spanish villagers, Bulgarian Gypsies and even the Russian Mafia have been reached with the gospel!

This is truly 'reality beyond reason', and, as you read this, my prayer would be that you too would realise that if we offer Him our *availability*, He can provide all necessary *ability* to achieve more than we could ever ask or imagine.

Examples of overseas folders

Greece

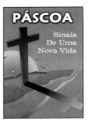
Portugal

Ukraine

Russia

Albania

Pakistan

Bulgaria

Guinea-Bissau

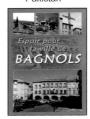
France

Burma

India

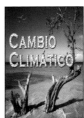
Spain

Poland

Hungary

Romania

Chapter 21

Special Projects

*'Go into all the world and preach the good news
to all creation.'*

Mark 16:15

Literature evangelism, by its very nature, is an undramatic,
unspectacular form of evangelism. And in a day when so few
will receive a clear understanding of the gospel in any other way,
at the very least it's a vital seed-sowing exercise. Christians
need to be spreading the gospel prayerfully, sensitively and with
urgency. After all, as it's been said, 'The gospel is only good
news to those who hear it in time'. But it's far more than mere
information sharing. Through this the Lord will change lives in
this world and secure eternal destinies for the next.

When one of our folders
is received it can take the
form of a link in a chain.
Sometimes it can be the
first link - the first time a
particular man, woman
or young person might
receive a presentation
of the gospel. On other
occasions it can be the
last link that the Lord uses
to bring the reader to
saving faith. Most times
however it's somewhere in between those two extremes.

Receiving a TELit folder at an open air market.

Much of the process of literature outreach can feel laborious
or monotonous or even of questionable value. However I
remember hearing an elderly missionary challenge this way
of thinking when he reminded his audience that, 'The heat
of the battle is in the slog!' So with this in mind, and given
the wonderful potential of the priceless message we present,
flagging zeal can be renewed and invigorated. After all, we

don't know how the Lord may be working in someone's heart. We have no access to the private, inner world of someone receiving one of our folders and, in the providence of God, even that which would appear to us to be unlikely in the extreme can be commonplace to Him. For example, a relative of one of the TELit Directors whilst working on the railway picked up a discarded tract and through this became a true believer.

If only more Christians would recognise the dynamic power of the Word of God under the direction of the Holy Spirit we might see many more professions of faith today. We need to liberate the Word that it might do the work for which it is intended, under the direction and power of the Holy Spirit. After all, outreach literature can travel further, say it better, last longer and cost less than just about every other form of evangelism:

> *'For in scattering divine literature we liberate thistledown laden with precious seed which, blown by the winds of the Spirit, floats over the world. The printed page never flinches, never shows cowardice, it is never tempted to compromise; it never tires, never grows disheartened; it travels cheaply, and requires no hired hall, it works while we sleep; it never loses its temper; and it works long after we are dead. The printed page is a visitor which gets inside the home, and stays there; it always catches a man in the right mood, for it speaks to him only when he is reading it; it always sticks to what it has said, and never answers back; and it is bait left permanently in the pool.'* **D.M.P.**

I've no idea who 'D.M.P.' is, but I reckon this is well worth pondering as the thrust of what the writer says is as relevant today as when it was first written.

SEIZING OPPORTUNITIES

It probably goes without saying that those of us involved in the work of TELit are advocates for the seizing of personal and corporate opportunities to spread the message of the gospel through our literature. Yet we also must be ready, not only to use the material ourselves, but to recognise and seize openings to

138

originate and develop new titles in order to exploit the potential of high profile events. And although a good proportion of our sales throughout each year is accounted for by the more general titles, there always seem to be specific events which justify some special project or other and which often constitute a significant proportion of overall sales.

The following is therefore a summary of some of these projects, each of which illustrates the principle asserted by one of the Puritans of old... *'Opportunity is the cream of time'*.

Northern Ireland 'Every Home' Project

Back in 1997 a man picked up a TELit folder in Belfast's Europa Hotel. He happened to be one of the leaders of The Ministry for Europe Trust, based in Holywood, Co. Down, and as a result TELit was approached regarding the prospect of an exciting project. This particular organisation wished to see an evangelistic publication placed in all 648,000 homes in Ulster, and asked TELit to design and produce a special folder for each of the six counties. (In fact, we ended up producing seven in total, with Co. Down split between North and South).

Each folder incorporated a special Freepost tear-off section designed to make it as easy as possible for those who wished further information or follow-up to be put into contact with those who initiated the project and could offer further help.

This proved a very worthwhile venture with well over 1,500 responding over the following years through the Freepost arrangement. Of course, as with a great deal of evangelistic activity of this nature, we'll never know this side of heaven just how much spiritual progress has actually been made through this particular project. And although by far most of the tangible responses were positive, we knew that such a large scale initiative would inevitably generate an aggressive backlash. For example, in the course of the Co. Antrim circulation I came into my office one day to find an *extremely* threatening message on my answering machine in a strong Northern Ireland accent! Mind you it's no new thing for me to be threatened in this way and it took me back to my days as an Inspector with the RSSPCC. Thankfully the threats in this particular message have not been carried out (so far) as I'm still alive and kicking!

EURO '96 Football Championship

The UK footballing fraternity has always been a 'hard to reach' sector of society when it comes to gospel communication. Therefore when it was decided that the Euro '96 Finals were to be held in England this seemed too good an opportunity to miss. We had already produced 'New Life United' which subsequently developed into 'The Winning Goal', but for this particular project I wanted to try a different approach.

DESIGN
Knowing that the matches in question were to be held at eight Premier League grounds and that many local football followers would attend their own stadium to watch the European teams in action, I wanted to 'localise' the appearance of each publication somehow. In so doing I hoped to capitalise upon the supporters' allegiance to their particular city and Club. Initially my idea was to produce eight separate designs featuring a photograph of each stadium on the front cover. But this proved too complicated. And even then, as a follower of football myself, I reckoned that a shot of some action would be much more interesting than a mere structure, though I realise that for some their team's stadium is virtually hallowed ground!

After much deliberation I decided to feature the same action shot in each version and use the local teams colours as a border. This was straightforward with Leeds and Newcastle but for the likes of Birmingham, Manchester and Sheffield some adaptation was required so as not to alienate a huge sector of footballing

General
Versions

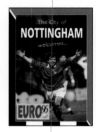   

Versions produced for specific locations.

devotees. The only way round this I felt was to split the borders between the two major teams in each city i.e., using the colours of Liverpool and Everton; Manchester United and Manchester City, etc. This seemed to work very well and added to the overall colour of the product.

FOLLOW-UP
This project was of course purely a TELit initiative and as such we had no particular client or clients who we knew would purchase these folders, so we decided to incorporate a

Freepost reply section with respondees directed to our office in Edinburgh. The idea was that TELit, with no particular church or denominational affiliation, would act as a clearing house. We would redirect responses to a network of Christians who were willing to offer follow-up. This group was drawn from those who would order significant quantities of folders and were thus demonstrating commitment to the project.

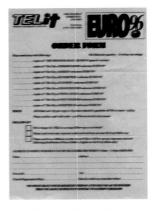

Our specially designed order form

So as to justify the considerable production outlay associated with this project, we needed to print a comparatively large quantity of folders or else the unit cost would be prohibitive. We fixed the retail price at 10p per folder, less discounts on bulk orders, which was really a very modest charge for this style of product. The final print run consisted of 30,000 copies of a basic version featuring the flags of all participating nations (mainly for use at the many large screen presentations up and down the country); a further 10,000 without a Freepost format for those who wished to organise their own follow-up, and then 10,000 copies for each of the eight main venues – a grand total of 120,000 copies.

RESPONSES

We publicised the project as widely as possible, and as the event drew near, orders began to flow in. Take-up was of course fairly uneven with some versions selling out completely whilst others were a bit more slow-moving. And although towards the end of the event small quantities had to be virtually given away as any left would be redundant, I'm pleased to say that all 120,000 were circulated throughout the UK.

Requests for follow-up arrived in the post each day and redirecting these to our network of contacts worked well. In all we received around 350 genuine responses, with only a few bearing an aggressive or obscene message. During the course of these Finals quite a number of tear-off cards were received with nothing on them at all. We can only assume that these were sent by those wishing to see us penalised financially.

Such malicious motivation was not totally unexpected, but it did sadden us nonetheless.

On a more positive note, although most responses were received from within the UK a number also came from different countries in Western Europe, including Scandinavia. Amazingly, responses were also received from as far afield as Lebanon, Baghdad and New Delhi. Two were received from fairly high profile Scottish professional footballers and we were contacted on several occasions by Christians telling us that they had given a copy of our publication to specific players prior to or following particular matches.

In an exercise such as this it's difficult to know exactly which responses are genuine and which are bogus. It's easy of course to discount those bearing the names of Mickey Mouse, Popeye and Man in the Moon! But we also received one in the name of the then Prime Minister, John Major, completed with his accurate address, including post code.

I subsequently wrote to him saying that I suspected this to have been completed and sent to us 'on his behalf'. But I went on to tell him that when considering the things of Eternity, one cannot be too careful, so therefore I was enclosing relevant follow-up material just in case. I received a very nice reply from him in due course confirming that this had indeed been a bogus response but that he appreciated our concern nevertheless.

This was an extremely expensive project due to the high origination and production costs, and yet TELit recovered financially from the inescapable outlay and at least we have the satisfaction of knowing that thousands of people have received the gospel who may not have been 'accessible' in any other way.

General Election 2001

With a General Election looming in 2001 we put together 'The POWER of the CROSS', a design intended to present the essence of the gospel through the UK political scene. My hope was that this would be used extensively in the run-up to the forthcoming Election but would also have some life expectancy well into the future. After all, politics in some shape or form does seem to dominate the news each day.

At an early stage in the production process my friend Robin, the then Assistant Secretary of Belfast City Mission, kindly arranged

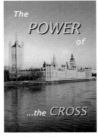  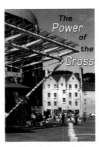

Original version   Reprinted version   Scottish version

a special launch of this particular publication using his Ulster Unionist contacts. It was held at Westminster on 31st January and hosted by M.P. Jeffrey Donaldson. Through this initiative each member of both Houses was given a copy of 'The POWER of the CROSS'.   And receiving an unexpected invitation to attend Prime Minister's Question Time was for me a real bonus.

Launch of 'The Power of the Cross' at Westminster

This evangelistic folder was greatly used throughout the 2001 Election period and has been reprinted on many occasions since then. To date we've seen 106,195 circulated throughout the UK

144

and in 2008 a special Scottish version was produced featuring shots of the Scottish Parliament Building.

The Cinema

Almost anything which commands large scale public attention is capable of forming the basis of a gospel publication. This includes films, and especially those which attract high profile publicity. In recent years three in particular have proved extremely useful in providing a platform for gospel literature outreach.

TITANIC
Winner of 11 Oscars in 1998, the Hollywood blockbuster movie *Titanic* seemed an obvious choice for such an approach. Although the film was an adaptation of the actual event back in 1912, the historical facts left me in no doubt that it would be worth developing the theme of a 'disaster waiting to happen'! After all, a direct parallel can be drawn between the fate of the ship and those of us who either ignore or reject the gospel.

When our publication became available this proved extremely popular, especially in Northern Ireland where the Titanic had been built. It gave me particular pleasure to design this folder because as a young apprentice joiner my paternal grandfather worked on the ship during its construction in Belfast. This became one of our best-selling general titles having been reprinted on no fewer than 15 occasions. Thus far we've had to produce a magnificent 177,800 copies, including 50,000 in Portuguese.

THE PASSION OF THE CHRIST
One of the most controversial films of recent times has been Mel Gibson's *The Passion of the Christ*.

As you'll no doubt remember it generated a great deal of strong feelings, both for and against, given its graphic portrayal of the world's first Easter weekend. I was privileged to attend a private screening for Christian leaders prior to its public release and this made an indelible impression upon me. But although the film left viewers in no doubt as to the 'how' of Christ's Passion, it was lightweight in terms of the 'why'. As I recall, much of the controversy centred on who was actually responsible for the death of the Lord Jesus Christ and accusations were made as to the film being anti-Semitic.

It was against this backdrop that we rather hurriedly put together 'The PASSION and the PROMISE' in which not only did we present the basics of the gospel but were at pains to emphasise the fact that neither the Romans nor the Jewish people had been responsible. Instead the Scriptures make it quite clear that it was the will of God the Father that His Son should suffer and die in order to satisfy His righteous wrath in the face of man's sin. The human authorities of the day were therefore little more than instruments in the hands of the One who was putting together the great 'Masterplan of Salvation'.

This particular publication has proved very popular since then, especially each Easter, and has been printed on 11 occasions so far selling a very respectable 154,300 copies, including 30,000 in Portuguese and 5,000 in Bulgarian. Feedback has also proved extremely encouraging and I remember a man phoning me to say he had become a true Christian having left the cinema and found a copy of our folder under the windscreen wiper of his car!

THE DA VINCI CODE

This became a massive best-selling novel and was followed by the film in 2006. It seemed to me that inherent within the storyline of what was, after all, only a work of fiction, lay a subtle and very dangerous deception. And this formed the theme of our publication.

146

The crucial element within the book and film centred upon the

identity of Jesus Christ. Through this its author called into serious doubt the deity of Christ, denying much of the Biblical account of His life, death and resurrection.

I'm not sure if this film went on to prove worthy of all the pre-release hype but it did give us the opportunity to produce a total of 60,000 copies of 'Da Vinci Deception', including 5,000 in Bulgarian.

British City Project

Those of us who have been Christians for any significant length of time might be surprised to realise just how much Biblical ignorance characterises our contemporary society. During my early years most of my friends and I attended Sunday School where we received at least some form of basic grounding in the Christian faith. But nowadays we can take none of this for granted and for this reason its vitally important not to make too many assumptions when it comes to presenting the basics of the gospel through evangelistic literature.

In years gone by, as can still be seen in some old style tracts, writers would freely use 'the language of Zion' to outline Biblical concepts. But today terms such as redemption, salvation, repentance and sanctification are no longer readily understood or indeed used by the man in the street. And as these are very serious spiritual issues it's vitally important that their meaning is clearly imparted.

You've probably heard it said that we must make the gospel relevant for today, but this is absolute rubbish! The gospel is *already* relevant, entirely relevant to everyone, but of course we've got to *demonstrate* that relevance or else many recipients will simply assume that Christianity is an outdated philosophy, okay perhaps for their granny, but not for them.

It's largely with this in mind that we've initiated our UK City project. In theory every centre of population can be used as a

BRITISH CITIES

Each one, a magnificent visual aid through which
the gospel can be presented.

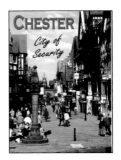

City of Security

City of Contradiction

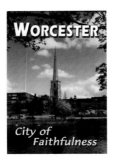

City of Faithfulness

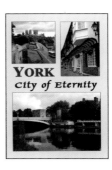

City of Eternity

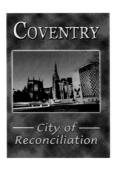

City of Reconciliation

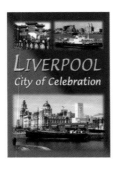

City of Celebration

City of Change

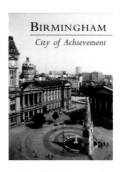

City of Achievement

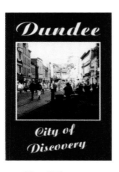

City of Discovery

148

form of visual aid for the gospel, especially cities. Each has a collection of unique features and we've tried to reflect this by identifying some clear characteristics through which the Christian gospel can be illuminated.

In this way many residents and visitors alike can receive a user-friendly evangelistic presentation. Portraying a particular city in a positive light, each design also explains the various elements of the gospel in practical, everyday terms.

The Sunday Times Rich List

With the publication by the *Sunday Times* of their 'Rich List' in 2003, I recognised the potential for an evangelistic initiative.

On the basis that each member of the List faced a lost Eternity unless they had been reconciled to God the Father through saving faith in Christ Jesus, we put together '..a better Investment'.

This would hopefully challenge all who were trusting in their material well-being to insulate themselves from the perils of contemporary living. No-one escapes 'the last enemy' and our hope was that at least some recipients might be made to question their own attitudes, values and spiritual situation while there was still time.

APPROACH

With production of '..a better Investment' underway, the next step was to do our best to find postal addresses for as many on the Rich List as possible. This proved quite difficult of course as many celebrities in particular proved extremely elusive, shunning publicity and no doubt thus avoiding begging letters! However, as a result of many hours with their noses stuck in Leith Library's copy of *Who's Who*, my youngest daughter Rebekah and her friend Roz came up with postal addresses for many hundreds, all of whom were then to receive a copy of our publication along with a carefully worded covering letter. In this way we (hopefully) saw a presentation of the gospel into the hands of many household names, including J. K. Rowling, Andrew Lloyd Webber, Madonna, Richard Branson and David Beckham.

FEEDBACK
We weren't sure if we'd receive any tangible response to this initiative and really didn't expect any. It was therefore to our surprise that we received two letters. Each was from a multimillionaire, one owned a top-flight football club and the other a well known business empire. Now it would be lovely to be able to report that these men had taken to heart the message of the gospel and found peace with God. But on the contrary, each was highly indignant. In fact, one clearly believed that in some way TELit was responsible for putting the Rich List together and he resented the idea that we should have anything to do with him and his money! On replying I made it clear that we had no link with the *Sunday Times* in any way and I agreed with him that no-one has the right to make any comment about him or his wealth. However I felt it important to remind each man that we will all be held accountable one day for how we've used the material well-being that has come our way.

CONCLUSION
I realise that we'll never know the true value of such an initiative this side of heaven, but with God's promise that His Word will not 'return to Him void' I feel sure that at least some will have been seriously challenged by the message. And reflecting upon the two very negative responses, I remember the words of a woman with whom I was working in my role as a 'Cruelty' Inspector back in the 70's. She told me that she would rather get a 'doin' from her man than be ignored by him. It may sound strange but in a similar way I would rather see someone respond to the gospel with aggression than indifference! A negative reaction shows to me that the issue in question has meant something of consequence to the person concerned and who knows how the Lord may yet intervene in someone's life. After all, there was a day when my sister Lenna told me that she would *never* become the kind of Christian I was, and now she travels the world with an international mission organisation, more on fire for the Lord than I am!

Robert Burns Bicentenary

Scotland's national poet Robert Burns died on 21st July 1796 at the age of 37. So it's perhaps no real surprise that in 1996, 200 years later, we at TELit considered his bicentenary a wonderful opportunity to create an evangelistic publication on the theme of his life.

Without exalting his well documented 'weaknesses', 'ROBERT BURNS More than a Legend' focused on the more positive characteristics of his life and became very popular throughout Ayrshire and Dumfries and Galloway in particular.

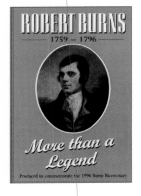

I had hoped that during the course of 1996 there might have been more interest from abroad, but publicising this publication proved quite difficult. Nevertheless, I was to hear of a very encouraging turn of events some months after the official bicentenary celebrations.

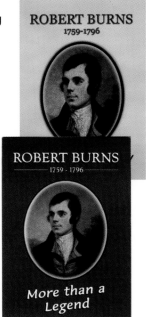

One day, whilst manning the TELit stand at a Christian Resources Exhibition in Glasgow, I was approached by a fellow who belonged to a Gospel Hall in Ayrshire. He and his friend had been distributing copies of our publication down at the Burns cottage in Alloway. It was the height of the celebrations, the building was covered in floral displays and visitors from all over the world had flocked to the site. Suddenly there was no small stir amongst the milling throng. It would appear that someone claiming to be a direct descendant of the Bard, and also bearing the name of Robert Burns, had turned up.

Well, did everyone not clamour for his autograph, yet few had anything on which to have him write. To their great surprise, before long a queue had formed in front of these two guys who were handing out 'More than a Legend'. They just couldn't give them away quickly enough and therefore many copies, now bearing the signature 'Robert Burns', would find their way all over the world, no doubt to become prized possessions. Little did most of these recipients know however that they were extending the life expectancy of our publication, thus enabling many others to read the priceless gospel of eternal salvation.

This particular folder has been reprinted on several further occasions and commands a regular slot in our catalogue, albeit with the reference to the bicentenary now removed.

The Gulf Wars

I don't know about you but I hate the prospect of war and yet I'm a firm believer in the concept of righteousness at any cost rather

than peace at any price. So when in 2003 the storm clouds began to gather over the Middle East and armed conflict appeared inevitable, I wondered if the Lord could in some way use TELit to bring the gospel message of love, reconciliation and peace to bear within prevailing circumstances.

I had the idea of using the developing Gulf crisis to emphasise the gulf that exists between man, in his natural state, and a holy God. As I do in all such situations, I committed the matter to the Lord in prayer. Over the years I've learned from experience that not every 'good idea' is from Him. However, on this occasion, the conviction that we ought to produce something continued to grow and I put together a design which picked up on the words of Matthew 24. The Lord Jesus Christ is speaking about the 'end times' and refers to the prospect of 'wars and rumours of wars'.

We produced an initial 10,000 copies, publicising these as widely as we could. And over a period of little more than a few weeks demand was such that we had to reprint on a number of occasions.

It's perhaps a sad reflection upon our world that this particular title is still seen as relevant to so many situations of conflict, and therefore '..wars and rumours of wars..' has become a popular general title within our catalogue. We know of many individuals, churches and Christian organisations who use it regularly and a number of copies have been sent to British troops serving in Iraq and Afghanistan. To date we've produced a total of 140,450 including 8,000 in Polish.

The Millennium

Most evangelistic opportunities appearing to justify the design of a specific evangelistic publication arise fairly quickly. But when it came to developing something for use in connection with the Millennium we certainly couldn't claim any shortage of lead-in time! Nevertheless we were still faced with the uncertainty of how best to 'exploit' this monumental milestone in human history.

We knew that every other Christian literature producer would be publishing their own booklets, brochures and tracts and it's never been our policy to simply duplicate the output of others. Therefore, after a good deal of prayerful deliberation, we came up with a three pronged approach.

'THE MILLENNIUM BUG When the chips are down in the year 2000'

As the year 2000 grew nearer, and in the face of all the public anxiety being expressed regarding a possible computer meltdown on a global scale, we recognised an outreach opportunity.

Developing a theme not too distant from that used in our 'Titanic' publication i.e., a disaster waiting to happen, 'The Millennium Bug' proved very popular as the 20th Century drew to a close. Needless to say of course the National Grid didn't seize up, nor did airliners plummet from the skies, but through all of this we were able to reach a potential minimum of 35,000 people with the gospel. Hopefully at least some would act upon the warning set out in this particular publication and thus avoid the greatest catastrophe of all - everlasting condemnation.

'Celebrating THE MILLENNIUM 2000 years of HIStory'

Given that our calendar here in the western world is fixed according to the birth of Jesus Christ, it would have been unthinkable not to have produced an evangelistic folder with Him as the central theme. This was despite the fact that many other Christian literature producers appeared to be thinking along similar lines. As we were soon to discover, a great number of churches both in the UK and overseas wanted to push the boat out and do something very special at this point in history. As a

 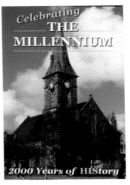 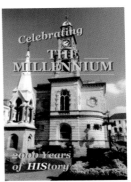

Basic version   Examples designed for specific churches

Polish   Russian   Spanish

154

result this particular publication was suddenly in great demand. We had to reprint it on no fewer than 22 occasions and ultimately went on to produce a staggering 493,455 copies, including versions in Spanish, Russian, German and Polish, as well as several which were custom-designed for individual churches.

This proved to have been one of the most significant projects in the history of TELit and the year 2000 saw us circulate more literature than in any other single year.

'CHRISTMAS MILLENNIUM'

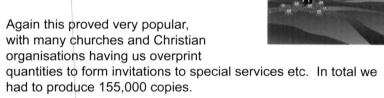

Our practice has been to produce a new Christmas folder each year. And for Christmas 1999, with the new Millennium approaching fast, we couldn't miss the opportunity to feature this in the context of Christmas.

Again this proved very popular, with many churches and Christian organisations having us overprint quantities to form invitations to special services etc. In total we had to produce 155,000 copies.

'Which Way?' Project

Back in the 1980's British evangelist Dick Saunders held his 'Way to Life Crusade' in a number of venues throughout the UK. And when this was brought to Edinburgh I was involved in counselling those who came forward to receive Christ Jesus each evening following the preaching of the gospel.

It occurred to me that whilst many appeared to make a valid profession of faith throughout this event, many others would remain a bit further upstream, challenged, but not yet ready to make a firm decision. To those in this position I felt it would have been helpful to have given a piece of literature briefly setting out the main elements of the gospel, as a form of reminder.

I had the idea of developing a publication with a play on the word

'Way', and although very simple in style it would be capable of presenting an overview of the gospel message. In fact, I've never felt it necessary to apologise for trying to simplify the gospel after hearing Billy Graham say that this was one of his greatest goals in life.

When I began to think the thing through it didn't seem too difficult to see real potential in this approach, for example:

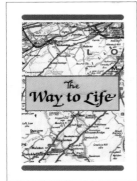

Pathway - *the pathway of life on which we all travel.*

Runway - *as Creator, God has the right to run our lives.*

Subway - *without God, our lives are 'less' than they should be.*

Waterway - *we have the tendency to 'water down' God's truth.*

This original design proved to be the forerunner of one of our most popular titles, 'Which Way?'

Railway - *without God we are 'off the rails'.*

Clearway - *God wants followers who will keep going.*

Freeway - *the cost of our salvation was paid at Calvary.*

Consequently, I put together a colour visual in the hope that Dick Saunders might be interested in my proposal. But, he wasn't, and I consigned the whole idea to the proverbial bin. However, although Dick didn't have sufficient enthusiasm to endorse this proposal, the project wasn't entirely the dead duck I considered it to be. I can't remember the precise circumstances, but 'Which Way?' was eventually printed in 1997 to sit alongside our other general titles. Since then it has been reprinted on many occasions with a total of 107,800 copies having been produced thus far.

Earlier in this book I paid tribute to others whose various forms of involvement in the work have proved vitally important. This is not limited of course to practical support but is also in terms of ideas and suggestions. These haven't always been taken up, but some have proved constructive in the extreme!

156

Within a year of 'Which Way?' having become available off the shelf, I was contacted by Belfast City Mission asking us if we could produce a special 'Belfast' version, were they to provide

A selection of the styles in which this folder has been produced.

relevant photographs. The project went ahead and the finished product became readily accepted on the streets of the city.

The relative ease with which this folder was produced - after all, it was just a question of adding the new photographs to the existing text and layout - led me to reckon we could offer this approach more widely. So long as others were willing and able to supply relevant photos and were prepared to accept our standard text we could provide a full colour gospel presentation for a particular place without having to charge a design fee.

From the client's point of view this was also an attractive option as it provided the opportunity to acquire custom-designed gospel literature featuring aspects of their local area at a fraction of the cost normally incurred. It also demanded a lot less brain power from me!

Over the years we've received orders for many places throughout the UK and beyond, and with a total of 504,560

'Which Way?'

Range of places for which a 'Which Way?' title has been produced - so far.

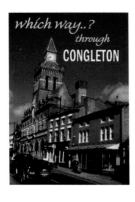

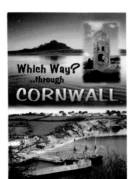

Arlesford	3,500
Anahilt	400
Ballykeel	3,000
Ballynafeigh	2,000
Bangor	5,000
Barton-on-Humber	5,000
Belfast	47,000
Bicester	24,000
Blackburn & Darwen	5,000
Boardmills	500
Brighton & Hove	5,000
Bristol	3,000
Buckingham	2,500
Cambridge	7,500
Carluke	6,000
Castledawson	3,000
Chatteris	2,500
Clanfield	3,000
Clevedon	3,000
Clonmel	10,500
Co Londonderry	45,000
Congleton	10,500
Cookstown	5,000
Cork & Kerry	10,000
Cornwall	18,980
Cullybackey	4,000
Curbar	200
Derby	8,880
Donemana	1,500
Drumlough	400
Duffield	2,000
Essex	10,000
Glencairn	2,000
Greenisland	2,500
Halifax	5,000
Hamilton	10,500
Hetton-le-Hole	2,500

'Which Way?'

Range of places for which a 'Which Way?' title has been produced - so far.

Kings Lynn	5,000
Kirkfieldbank	1,000
Larne	15,000
Leeds	7,500
Leyland	3,000
Lisburn	12,000
Lisburn Road	2,000
LLandudno	3,000
Loughor	2,500
Lurgan	5,000
Moira	2,000
New Cross	2,500
Nidderdale	2,500
Ormskirk	3,000
Orrell	3,500
Otley	3,500
Perth	5,000
Peterborough	56,200
Pontefract	1,000
Portadown	6,000
Poyntzpass	1,000
Rathcoole	3,000
Ripon	5,000
Sandy Row	3,000
Scarborough	10,000
Southampton	10,000
Stockport	4,500
Stoke-on-Trent	7,000
Teesdale	5,000
The Borders	3,000
The Shankill	4,000
The Sperrins	1,500
Thirsk	9,000
Tottenham	10,000
Winchester	7,000
Wokingham	5,000
Woolpit	5,000

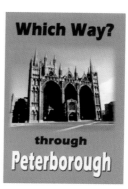

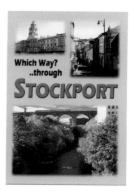

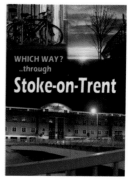

copies produced thus far, this has certainly proved to have been an inspired initiative - one to which my contribution was pretty minimal.

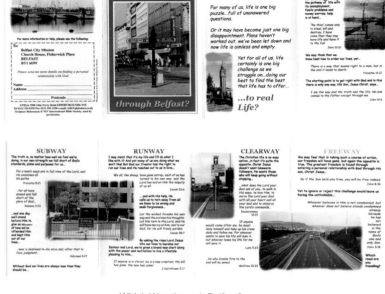

Which Way through Belfast?

Every Home in Scotland for Christ

I can't remember exactly how it happened but in 2006 I came across a publication being circulated by this particular Charitable Trust based in Glasgow. It was a gospel tract accompanied by a reply-paid post card. I went on to discover that the objective was to circulate these across the country, thus reaching every home for Christ.

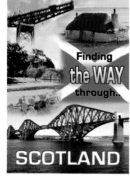

I really warmed to the vision and enterprise of these folks but felt that TELit could design and

160